FAITH
WALKING
with
JESUS

FAITH WALKING

with

JESUS

ELMER L. TOWNS

DESTINY IMAGE® PUBLISHERS, INC.
P.O. Box 310, Shippensburg, PA 17257-0310
"Promoting Inspired Lives."

This book and all other Destiny Image and Destiny Image Fiction books are available at Christian bookstores and distributors worldwide.

For more information on foreign distributors, call 717-532-3040.

Reach us on the Internet: www.destinyimage.com.

ISBN 13 TP: 978-0-7684-7174-8

ISBN 13 eBook: 978-0-7684-7175-5

For Worldwide Distribution.

1 2 3 4 5 6 7 8 / 27 26 25 24 23

CONTENTS

BEGINNING YOUR FAITH WALK

As you have accepted Christ Jesus by faith,
continue to faith-walk in Him.

Colossians 2:6, ELT

IF you could speak all the languages used around the world, and you complimented God with the most beautiful and wonderful words known by mankind, but you did not have faith—faith in God—you would not go to live with God when you die.

If you were the richest person in the world, owned a number of businesses, homes, vehicles and planes, and if you used your money to build universities with free tuition for anyone wanting an education, and you could wipe out hunger, and could provide shelter for all needing a roof over their heads, but you did not have God's faith in your heart, you would not accomplish anything for eternity.

If you were the nicest person on Earth, and you complimented anyone and everyone on their strengths while overlooking their faults, and you could counsel and guide people through the obstacles destroying their life, and if everyone considered you the perfect/ideal person, but you did not tell them about your faith in God, did not influence others, your advantage would be meaningless.

Those who have God's faith believe He exists, and when you have that faith it puts you into a relationship with the Lord God who created the universe. You gained that intimate fellowship with the Father when you accepted Jesus Christ as your Savior from sin. Your faith grants you access into God's presence, and only you and all others who come by faith in Christ can get the Father's attention so that He listens to your needs/requests and answers you.

Your faith got the attention of a holy God, who created hell to punish all who refuse to approach Him by faith. Your God will see your faith in His Son and will open the benefits of Heaven to you, because your faith gives you a righteous standing before Him—the Almighty Father God.

Faith can do for you what you cannot do for yourself. Your faith has the potential to make you wiser than you are; it has the potential to make you more spiritual ... more humble ... more understanding of others ... wiser to make decisions ... smarter to be a better family member or parent. Faith has the potential to do for you what you dream ... or desire ... or work for ... or what God has planned for your life (see Jeremiah 29:13).

Your faith has the potential to give you victory over pressure ... persecution ... and even torture. Your faith will transform your personality so you live for other people ... who live for society and government, and you will be a loyal citizen of your nation. But most of all, you will do it by the faith God gives you.

Your faith makes you loving ... kind ... patient, and not selfish. People will like you because your faith focuses on others first, before taking care of the needs of self.

All your rewards and accomplishments will pass away, people will forget your good deeds, and no one will remember the things you owned—cars, houses, businesses, etc.—and they will forget all your accomplishments. But your faith will guide you through this life, and your faith will give you access to Heaven when you die, and your faith will gain you the righteous standing only attained by Jesus Christ. And you can have that position because you stand in Jesus Christ. Then God the Father will look at you to see the perfection of His Son.

People without Jesus look at the world through imperfect eyes. They see things they cannot fully understand and many things in life puzzle them. They don't know the answers to the mysteries of living nor the purpose of life.

When they were children, they learned things from experience, and they looked at everything through the eyes of childhood. Most were happy and most kept learning. But they passed from childhood into adulthood. Then they did not know everything and could not do everything, nor go anywhere they wanted, and could not have everything they desired. Adult desires are different from childhood desires.

But faith never changes. The simple faith of a child is enough to gain Heaven, and the exciting faith of teen years opens doors. The mature faith of adults is the compass to point your life into a meaningful course. Old people found their faith was the rudder that helped them find their way to the heavenly Father.

When I was a child I thought I saw things perfectly—according to my limited measurement of life. But my faith gave me spiritual eyes to see my sin, and to see Christ dying for my sin ... and my faith showed me the way to Heaven through Jesus. My imperfect childhood eyes gave me confidence and assurance. But then I became an adult and I now see my imperfections more plainly. I see the faults of others, and I see some who never try to please God, but their imperfections are evident to me, imperfections I did not see as a child.

But when I look at adult life through *faith eyes*, I see a way to please God ... and serve God ... and be used by God ... and a way to glorify God. My adult faith eyes help me look at the world the way God sees it. God shows me what to do and how to do it. Then God can use me to make a difference—although a small difference—even when there is so much evil and destruction everywhere.

So I get up every morning with my faith and what I call faith eyes. I let my new eyes guide me through the day. And when I get ready to sleep at night, I use my faith eyes to pray to thank God for a good day ... to ask Him to forgive my sins as I forgive those who sinned against me ... and to give me strength to resist temptation.

Then I go to sleep in Jesus, because one day I will actually do it. And when I wake up, I will be with Jesus, which is my total purpose in life.

Introduction

LEARNING FAITH-WALKING

"FAITH" is one of the most difficult words in the English language to understand and put into action. It should be the easiest word because Jesus simply told some listeners, "Have faith in God" (Mark 11:22).

But think about the Buddhists, who say Buddha is God, and they say, "Have faith in Buddha." What about the Muslims, who say Allah is God, so they tell us, "Have faith in Allah." But can Buddha and Allah save a person from eternal damnation?

Must faith be in a specific god? Also, must faith be expressed in certain words or expressions or symbols? Or should faith reflect a certain attitude or response of the individual's heart when searching for God?

This book is about faith-walking. It answers the question, what is walking by faith? It also answers, who can walk by faith and how can it happen? Can anyone walk by faith if they don't know what faith means?

Even Webster's Dictionary gives several definitions of "faith": "Faith, (1) to trust, i.e., allegiance to duty or a person; (2) a promise; (3) belief and trust in, and loyalty to God; (4) a firm belief in something for which there is no proof; (5) belief in the traditional doctrines of a religion; (6) something that is believed with strong convictions; (7) a system of religious beliefs."

To help answer the question "what is faith?" chapter 1 will give a definition of "faith" found in the Bible. It begins with doctrinal faith (objectual, i.e., Scripture) and reaches to saving faith (your inner response to the Word of God).

But even in the correct definition of faith, true faith is not something that agrees with the dictionary, or agrees with your understanding, or even pleases the leaders of your church or the doctrine of your church. Your faith must please God, and if it doesn't please God, it doesn't matter; and it will not help you in this life or give you entrance to the next. "Without faith it is impossible to please God" (Hebrews 11:6).

Next, this book explains why you need both faith and works, for one without the other will not work. Just as a bird must have two wings to fly, so you must have both faith and works to get off the ground. You will crash when you try to fly with one but not the other.

But sometimes to get off the ground you must use both together, i.e., faith and works. The third chapter is called "A Leap of Faith." It is not enough to know about faith, or to feel faith with your emotions, or just rely on your works. No, not at all. You must make a leap of faith into God's waiting arms so He can use you ... lead you ... empower you ... or save you.

But then when you are ready to use your faith to walk with God, or get answers to prayer, then you rest in God's gift of faith that He has given you. The greatest of all spiritual gifts is faith ... faith to serve God ... faith to be used by God ... faith to accomplish great things for God— even move mountains.

The last chapter in this book should be the first: "How to Grow Your Faith." When you get saved by faith, you use your faith to worship God

... follow God ... please God ... and be faithful to God. So the last should be first, but you cannot appreciate and apply faith until you have learned all the above lessons about faith. It is then that you are ready to grow your faith. And how do you grow faith? Like any and all other Christian virtues. But since faith is more vital than all other virtues, because they are built on faith, then this last chapter is the important one. You have not finished this book about faith until you know how to protect ... nurture ... and grow your faith.

This book is about faith-walking. Not faith running, not faith standing. But walking by faith moment by moment ... daily.

Don't just read this book to know about faith. Begin walking it constantly. And how can you do that? Look at the daily devotionals. They are written to instruct you how to faith-walk. But more than that, these daily devotions will urge you to try faith-walking.

Remember when you were small and could not stand without help? Then one day a parent let go and you stood by yourself? That was the greatest achievement in your life up to that moment. But you did it; you stood alone.

Next a parent held out their arms and invited you to "come." You did it by yourself. One step after another ... you walked. You would not have walked without a parent ... without encouragement ... without their release giving you freedom to walk. This book encourages you to let go and walk to please your heavenly Father. Remember, "faith ... pleases God" (Hebrews 11:6).

Faith-walking—every babe in Christ is designed by God to faith-walk. Remember, some in the Bible are called "babies" and we know a baby cannot walk. According to Hebrews 5:11-16, babies need more than milk; they need the nourishment of solid food to grow strong enough to walk. Look in Scripture to see the other ways to faith-walk. We are to light-walk (see 1 John 1:7) and Jesus-walk, i.e., we are to "walk, even as He [Jesus] walked" (1 John 2:6).

THINGS ABOUT FAITH-WALKING

1. What is the importance of faith-walking?

There are two important actions in faith-walking: the first is faith and the second is walking. Obviously, faith is the first because (1) faith is believing or trusting God, and (2) faith gives purpose to your walk. Both words, "faith" and "walking," are important. If you don't have both faith and walking, then you have neither. Because when you have faith, it is manifested in actions, i.e., walking. And when you are walking, you are guided by an inward power —faith. "Without faith it is impossible to please God" (Hebrews 11:6).

Which is more important of the two words? Obviously walking is the most important because some in the Bible had faith but it was dead faith. Doesn't Scripture tell us that "faith without works is dead" (James 2:26)? So your faith is nothing if it is not connected to works/walking.

So every time you think faith, automatically realize it is faith-walking. And every time you think of walking or following Jesus Christ, you are putting your faith into action.

So, what is the conclusion? If you have genuine faith in Jesus Christ, then you will walk/follow Him. And if you are trying to live out the Christian life by walking, then you are expressing faith in Jesus. If you don't have both, then you don't have either. Both need each other, and both find their meaning in each other.

2. What motivated faith-walking?

When you are faith-walking, you are not standing still ... waiting ... sitting ... or even standing on your tiptoes. No! Faith-walking is movement ... action ... change ... growth ... moving toward a destination.

Faith-walking involves learning how to walk better ... faster ... and more safely. Also, faith-walking is leaving a past experience ... a past location ... a past time in your life ... or leaving yesterday. Faith-walking is about where you are going ... the future ... the next destination in life ... the horizon ... the next challenge.

3. When can you begin faith-walking?

The answer is obviously *now*! You can take your first step of faith—*now*! If you are not a Christian and you don't follow Jesus Christ, you can make a decision to faith-walk *now*!

First, realize you are a sinner (see Romans 3:23) and cannot please God while in your sins. Then realize God must punish all sin and sinners, because He is the holy God who allows no one who is a sinner to approach Him (see Romans 6:23). But there is a way or solution to this problem. Jesus died to forgive your sins (see Romans 5:8) and cleanse you from sins that condemn you (see Romans 10:9-10). When you repent of your sins and reach out to God, Jesus Christ comes into your heart and life (see John 1:12). When you get Jesus, you get forgiveness ... cleansing ... because Jesus enters your life.

It is an act of faith the moment you believe in your heart and receive Jesus Christ into your life. Immediately you enter a new relationship with God. He is your heavenly Father, and you have a new obligation to believe in Him ... obey Him ... please Him ... and walk in faith. You begin immediately faith-walking when you are saved. If you are a Christian and are not faith-walking, then begin *now*! What does God want you to do? Begin *now*!

4. What kind of believer can faith-walk?

People just born again can take infant steps of faith because they are babes in Christ. Faith-walking is obeying Jesus ... looking to Jesus

... stepping toward Jesus. The new Christian can faith-walk, so can the older Christian (older in spiritual age and older in physical age). Both can faith-walk. Backslidden Christians can begin faith-walking by turning to Jesus, confessing their sin, then reaching out to the Savior and stepping out toward Him.

5. How old must you be to faith-walk?

You can know about God and the way He runs the world as you begin to learn all about life. Then you can learn how God invites you to be His child. You can believe and begin faith-walking when you learn about Him and you make the God of the universe your heavenly Father. How young? If you are old enough to know the love of both God the Father and Jesus, then you are old enough to believe in Jesus. Now you are old enough to faith-walk.

PART ONE

FAITH
WALKING
with
JESUS

Chapter 1

GETTING
BIGGER FAITH

I think Jerry Falwell had the greatest faith of any individual I have ever met. Falwell planted and built Thomas Road Baptist Church in Lynchburg, Virginia, to an attendance of around 10,000 weekly. Not only that, but he was also founder of Liberty University in 1971, and 50 years later the university has over 120,000 students and a budget of $1.2 billion. Also, he founded Moral Majority, a powerful political/religious lobbying group that was responsible for putting Ronald Regan into the White House in 1982.

I asked Jerry, "How did you get such great faith?"

"I don't have great faith," Jerry answered me.

I was a little disappointed with his answer. I didn't know what to say and was sitting there with questions in my mind. Then he said, "I don't have great faith, but I faith in a great God." Then he went on to explain, "It's not great faith that gets great answers to prayers; it's our great God who responds to our faith."

So my next question was very obvious: "When did you find this faith in a great God, or how did you get it?"

Jerry told me about enrolling in Baptist Bible College, Springfield, Missouri, in 1956. His mother had bought him a brand-new Plymouth sedan for $4,000. That made him the talk of the campus.

Jerry had been saved the previous year in a soul-winning Baptist church in Lynchburg, Virginia. That church motivated him to serve God. His pastor told him when he got to Springfield to attend High Street Baptist Church and find a Sunday school class and teach it. So Jerry found and asked the Sunday school superintendent for a class. He was a layman with a hardened fundamentalist mentality. He viewed Jerry skeptically but said to him, "I don't have a class open, but you can start one next week." The potential class of fifth-grade junior boys met with one boy named Darryl.

After the Sunday school opening exercise in the church basement, the students went into their assigned classrooms, surrounding the auditorium. Jerry's class met in the corner of the big auditorium where a few chairs had been placed. Jerry taught Darryl and challenged him, "Bring a friend next week."

The same thing happened the second week, only Darryl was present, and he once again said, "Bring a friend next week." The third week the same thing happened.

The following Saturday Jerry drove his Plymouth to pick up Darryl and challenged him, "Let's find every fifth-grade boy in town and invite him to Sunday school."

Faced with failure, Jerry heard a challenging message during a college chapel. His answer to a failing Sunday school class was God. He heard stories of great heroes of the faith who prayed ... trusted God ... and their faith moved mountains (see Mark 11:22-23). Jerry thought, *Why not me?*

Jerry got the key to an empty luggage room in his college dorm and went in right after lunch each day to pray for his class to grow ... for power ... for God to do a miracle. He found it difficult to keep praying longer than an hour, so he went to the college librarian, who supplied him with deeper life books on praying, fasting, and the "crucified life."

Jerry began praying for himself before he prayed for the class. He asked God for the faith of Adoniram Judson, William Carey, Dwight L. Moody, Billy Sunday, and George Müller. These Christian leaders did outstanding work—pioneering ministry—and Jerry wanted their faith.

The secret for the growth of Jerry's Sunday school class was found in his afternoon prayer times. For the whole year, Jerry spent every afternoon in prayer, reading great books and growing his faith.

Jerry went to Darryl's home on Saturday morning; "Let's go get all your friends." They expanded their vision to visit and invite every fifth-grade boy in the city to the class. The class averaged 53 in attendance each week and over 100 boys on special promotion days.

VISION OF A NEW UNIVERSITY

I was teaching at Trinity Evangelical School in greater Chicago, Illinois, when God worked in my spirit to teach in an aggressive soul-winning college to train young people to build great soul-winning churches. Trinity was a great seminary with outstanding academic credentials. Its faculty was recognized in the evangelical world, but I wanted to be part of an aggressive ministerial training college/seminary that could change the world for Christ.

I interviewed for a position at Baptist Bible College with its president, Beauchamp Vick, pastor of Temple Baptist Church, Detroit, Michigan, the fourth largest in the world at that time; and Pastor Parker

Daily of Kansas City, chairman of the board at Baptist Bible College. They offered me a position to teach in the fall of 1971. This was the college where Jerry Falwell's life was transformed.

I felt God had answered my prayer and was looking forward to going to Baptist Bible College, a challenging, growing ministerial training center.

But everything changed on the last Sunday in January 1971. I preached at Canton Baptist Temple, Canton, Ohio, where Pastor Harold Henninger had planted and built the seventh largest church in America. Henninger was on the board of trustees at the Baptist Bible College and I thought he would be happy when I told him I would teach at Baptist Bible College. But to my surprise he said, "Oh no Elmer ... that is a mistake." Then with a sober face he said, "I know that you are a committed evangelical, and you want to train people, but that school is a fundamentalist school and they are not open to having evangelicals teach on their faculty." Henninger shook his head and then added, "You will be fired before the first semester is up."

Needless to say, my dream and world fell apart. I stood there not knowing what to say. Then Henninger said to me, "Jerry Falwell is going to start a college in his church." At the time Falwell had planted and built the tenth largest Sunday school in America and had an aggressive soul-winning church. Henninger said to me, "You and Falwell are like two peas in a pod. Go start a college for him. Together you two can change the world." Quite a challenge.

I went back to my motel room, located in the church Sunday school facilities, and picked up the phone to dial Jerry Falwell's number. I did not know what I was going to say to him, or how I would begin the conversation. We were friends and I had interviewed him because his church was in the book *Ten Largest Sunday Schools in America*, a best-selling book.

"Hello ... this is Elmer Towns."

"Dr. Towns ... what do you want to call the college?" Jerry said.

I was flabbergasted. "You don't start with the name of the college; you start with its purpose."

So Falwell said, "So tell me the purpose of this new college you will start for me." For the next hour I outlined my vision of an aggressive soul-winning ministerial college that could change the world.

I described the college as a three-legged stool. I painted a mental picture: "The first leg would be *academic excellence*. I want our college to be greater than most Bible colleges; our college would be a liberal arts college."

"No ... not liberal," Jerry reacted; the term "liberal" was hated by fundamentalists. I explained that the term "liberal arts" meant a broad college curriculum to teach the arts and sciences. I said we'd train educators, businessmen, and engineers, not just people for ministry.

"We'll even start a law school."

In those days, Wheaton College was committed to academic excellence, but it had co-ed dorms, so I said, "We don't want to compromise like Wheaton, but we want to build a college with *academic excellence* like Wheaton."

"The second leg of the stool is *cutting-edge creativity*," I explained. "Our college will be culturally relevant and streamlined to the times." I wanted our college to minister in a world of computers and television, just like his church. In those days, Falwell thought Bob Jones University was the most creative in outreach. I said to Jerry, "Let's be as creative as Bob Jones, but let's not be swallowed up by legalism." He agreed.

"The third leg of the stool is *local church evangelism*." We both agreed that Baptist Bible College, Springfield, Missouri, was one of the greatest places to train pastors for ministry because of its involvement with evangelism through local churches. I explained, "Let's be evangelistic like Baptist Bible College, but let's not adopt its 'hillbilly' ways."[1]

Jerry agreed to the concept of a three-legged stool. Then I added, "I've got another innovation for our college that would be world changing." I explained that I didn't want to start a school controlled by a denomination, or church fellowship, such as Baptist Bible College. Also, I didn't want an independent college with its own board of directors, such as Bob Jones and other independent schools.

I explained to Jerry my idea: "A Christian college should be the extension of a local church at the collegiate level: everything a church does to influence its people to evangelism, the Christian college should also do to influence its students, but at a college or university level." I told Jerry we would start a college where all of our students would be members of Thomas Road Baptist Church, did their Christian service in the church, and the spiritual dynamics of Thomas Road Baptist Church would infuse spiritual life into the college.

"I love that idea," Jerry agreed. Then he said, "Elmer, of course you'll be president." He was assuming that since I had been a Bible college president, I would run the college.

"Absolutely not." Jerry was shocked by my response.

I had come to the conclusion in Canada that "great men build great colleges; average men build average colleges." That night I called Jerry a modern-day Charles Spurgeon, the pastor who built the most powerful Protestant church in London when England ruled the world.

"Don't compare me to Spurgeon," Falwell argued.

"You did something few have done," I explained. "You started your own church and built it into one of the largest in America." In addition, Jerry had built a television empire across America. I felt the new college should be as large as the talents and faith of Jerry Falwell. My opinion that night has been confirmed by the modern-day Liberty University.[2]

ONE WOMAN PRAYED
WHILE WE PLANNED

I didn't know it until after our phone call was over, but fifteen minutes prior to my calling Jerry, he had called my home in greater Chicago and had talked to my wife, Ruth. He told my wife that he wanted me to start a college because he liked my spirit and vision, commenting, "Elmer gets things done!" After talking with Ruth a few minutes, Jerry said, "I never ask a wife if her husband would come work for me, but do you think that Elmer would come start a college for me?"

"He'd be perfect for the job," Ruth answered Jerry. She explained that I had been a college president in Winnipeg, and I had been on the national committee to set college standards of the AABC, the Accrediting Association of Bible Colleges. As they continued talking, he sold Ruth on the college before talking with me. As a result, Ruth immediately began praying for the college, asking God to motivate me to phone her long-distance so she could tell me about the new college. For an hour, while Jerry and I were drawing mental blueprints for a world-changing college, Ruth was in the presence of God interceding for our future. God's timing for spiritual advances is always perfect.

HOW MANY STUDENTS?

Jerry Falwell asked me how many students we would have the first year at this new college. I told him that Bob Jones University and Tennessee Temple University each had 3,000 students. Then Jerry said with faith to me, "Let's think about 5,000 students as our goal." That was bigger than I had ever expected and required more faith than I had ever had.

Liberty University began with 154 students that first year, more than we ever expected to attend. So, again Jerry asked me, "How many students do you think we will eventually have?" I answered him, "You said 5,000." Now Jerry said, "Now I am thinking about 50,000 students." The following year Jerry came to me and said, "I want to change my goal; we are going to have 100,000 students."

Today Liberty University has 120,000 students and a financial budget of $1.2 billion a year—more than I ever thought could happen. Jerry had faith for the impossible and believed it, preached it, and prayed for it, as we worked for it.

FAITH PRODUCED A $5 MILLION MIRACLE AND SEVEN DORMITORIES

In 1978, Liberty University was seven years old and attendance had reached 4,000 students. But for the coming year, Jerry planned on 5,000 students. To accommodate that many students, seven dormitories were built on the small hill overlooking the campus, located next to the prayer chapel. Liberty had contracted for the seven three-story dormitory buildings, which would accommodate around 1,000 students, but the money had run out and the contractors shut the job down. Over the winter, weeds had grown up around the property, and water, dust, and debris filled the bottom of the construction sites. The walls were up, the roofs were in place, but seven empty buildings were a testimony to our empty faith. Five million dollars were needed to pay off the construction company and finish the project.

On a warm spring day Jerry walked into the university chapel to announce, "We are not having chapel in here today. We are all going to walk out that door"—pointing to the road leading up to the seven buildings. "I want all of us —4,000 students—to walk around the buildings seven times, then kneel down in groups of seven to ask God for $5 million. We must have that money so we can have dorm rooms for an additional 1,000 students this fall."

When Jerry jumped off the platform, I was the first to follow him ... out the door, down the road, and around the unfinished buildings. There were seven faculty in the small circle surrounding Jerry Falwell and me.

I prayed first: "Lord, I don't have faith for $5 million, but I believe You answer prayer. So, Lord, I am asking: give me faith to finish these dorms."

All the other faculty in the circle prayed; then Jerry confidently told God, "Lord, You have a lot of money and I need some of it." Then he asked in faith, "Lord, I am going to tell the workmen to start next Monday. That means the following Friday I need the first payment to meet paychecks, or the workers will walk off the job and we will never finish." He concluded, "Lord, touch the hearts of people to start mailing in money today, and keep it coming in week after week until we get the students in those dorms."

God recognized Falwell's faith and answer his prayer. Five months later, Liberty reached 5,000 students and all the dorms—including the seven new ones—were occupied at the beginning of that school year. The money came in week by week, one mail delivery after another. People all over America had watched on television the students and Jerry walking around the buildings and claiming them. Because Jerry's prayer had been televised, people heard him pray and began sending in money.

In the early days, Liberty took financial steps that caused financial problems. Some would call them foolish steps; others would call them steps of faith. But money was spent that the university did not have, expecting God to supply. So in 1992, Liberty faced bankruptcy. What worked before, spending money, depending on God to send it in, did not work this time.

Two major national financial crises hurt the university's income. First, there was a financial recession in 1988, influencing all industry and businesses, and the university had not completely gotten over that. Also, in 1985, television preacher Jim Bakker had a financial scandal at the television ministry of PTL in Charlotte, North Carolina. Thousands of Christian people lost millions of dollars they had invested in the leader's dream. Giving to Christian ministries declined at all faith institutions, including Billy Graham, and major Pentecostal broadcasters, including Jerry Falwell and Liberty University. The public lost confidence in giving to any television ministry, and that was Liberty's main source of income. Liberty found itself $104 million in debt.

Liberty not only faced bankruptcy, but also many lending institutions that had provided loans to Liberty filed legal claims against the university and were threatening to take over operations of the university. Over the years, many individuals had left various assets to Liberty University, including property, stocks, bonds, and other forms of annuities. The financial team at Liberty University had begun selling off these assets to pay our indebtedness. That reduced the total indebtedness to $52 million. We had nothing left to liquidate and nothing else to do. Jerry Falwell went on a 40-day fast asking God for $52 million.

I remember walking into the church back room one Sunday morning and saying to Jerry, "It looks like you have lost a lot of weight."

"This is not weight loss. I am on a 40-day fast and I am 25 days into the fast," Jerry told me.

That Sunday morning he announced to Thomas Road Baptist Church that he was on a fast and asked that everyone pray for him and with him, because he was asking God for $52 million.

At the end of the 40 days, the money did not come in. Liberty still faced bankruptcy and financial disaster and the loss of everything. Jerry began eating and did so for the next 25 days. He began putting on weight and regaining his health.

The money had not come in; Liberty still faced the $52 million indebtedness. The property was going to be taken from the university and there would be no school the following year. Jerry went on a second 40-day fast. I remember warning him, "Jerry, you look terrible ... this will kill you."

Jerry replied, "I don't mind spiritual death. I would give my life for Liberty University." But Jerry explained that it was more than dying spiritually; it was dying to get God's life. He was willing to die physically and spiritually to get God's answer. Would God honor his request?

A couple days after his second 40-day fast was over, Jerry phoned me around 1:30 in the afternoon. "Get up to my office quick. You will see a miracle today that is bigger than anything you will see again in your life." I knew that was good news. Immediately I hung up the phone and took off in a fast walk up to Jerry's office.

There were about ten of the university leaders all sitting in his office waiting. Jerry announced, "A courier is coming from A. L. Williams. You will see a miracle today. God will answer our prayers and we will all see the great work God is doing for Liberty."

The courier had flown to Lynchburg on a chartered jet, then he walked into Jerry's office to give him two parcels. The first contained a check for $25 million. Jerry walked around the room showing it to each one of us.

"I want to hold it," I said to Jerry, reaching out for the check.

"No ... no one touches this until I hand it to Mr. Carter at the Carter Bank and Trust Company." That was where Liberty did all of its banking, and Carter was the president of the bank.

There were several parcels of paper in the second package, some twelve inches thick. Each group of papers represented various bills, invoices, mortgages, and technical financial papers. Jerry and the board would sign all those papers transferring the indebtedness of Liberty

University over to A. L. Williams and the various organizations in his financial empire. Jerry went on to explain that many of the loans that we had taken out had such low interest rates that A. L. Williams wanted to take advantage of those low-interest rate loans. In one afternoon, Liberty was out of debt!

Today, Liberty has a campus worth $1.2 billion and has no debt. Because Liberty has been very careful in managing its income, the university has cash in banks in Toronto and Montreal, Canada, and the Bahamas. Enough cash to run the university for five years if our nation and the world go into financial depression.

God honored the faith of Jerry Falwell. That included the prayers of many people, including faculty, students, and prayer partners all around the world who prayed and believed God would do miracles for Liberty University.

But remember, Jerry had said, "I don't have great faith ... I have a great God." God can do the miraculous.

NOTES

1. The pejorative term "hillbilly" is a put-down by those prejudiced for cosmopolitan ways. That night I used this term to suggest we would teach classical music and drama, not just Southern Gospel. I used that term to suggest the new college would position itself to serve all of evangelical Christianity, not just the narrow section served by Baptist Bible College.

2. Liberty University had two previous names in the early years. First it was called Lynchburg Baptist College, and second was Liberty Baptist College, but in this book it will be called by its present name, Liberty University, because that identification is in the minds of most people.

Chapter 2

SIX EXPRESSIONS OF FAITH IN SCRIPTURE

FAITH CATEGORIES

THE Bible lists six categories, or expressions, of faith, suggesting you can begin with initial faith, which is the content of faith found in the Bible. Then you can grow to a deeper experience of faith, which can be living by faith, or the indwelling faith of Jesus Christ, who lives within your life. Faith is both a noun, which is a statement of faith, and a verb, which has action.

SIX EXPRESSIONS OR CATEGORIES OF FAITH

1. Statement of faith, i.e., content

2. Saving faith, our action/response that leads to salvation

3. Justifying faith, non-experiential faith that declares us righteous

4. Indwelling faith, the power in Jesus Christ that lives in us

5. Living by faith, daily experience

6. The spiritual gift of faith, an ability to serve God

1. *Statement of faith.* The first step in understanding faith is to know the content of faith. When the Bible uses the definite article "the" with the word "faith," it means a statement of faith or the doctrinal content of faith. According to James I. Packer, "'the faith' denotes the body of truths believed (e.g., Jude 3; Romans 1:5; Galatians 1:23; 1 Timothy 4:1, 6). This became standard usage in the second century."[1] There is objectivity in Christianity, and the Christian life is based on the objective Word of God. The basis or foundation of living the Christian life is to know the content and/or principles of Scripture, then applying it to your daily experience. The more you know your faith, the better you can live by faith.

2. *Saving faith.* A person experiences conversion, also called saving faith. This is when they apply the content of faith to their life and they trust in Christ for salvation. "For by grace are ye saved through faith" (Ephesians 2:8, KJV). Personal salvation is an experience that involves

the response of the total person (personality: intellect, emotions, and will) to God.

Note how the total personality is involved in a conversion experience. First, a person's mind must know the gospel (see 1 Corinthians 15:1-3); he must know he is a sinner (see Romans 3:23); and he must know the punishment awaiting sin (see Romans 6:23). Second, the positive emotions are involved in love for God (see Matthew 22:37), and negative emotions are involved in remorse for sin, "For godly sorrow worketh repentance to salvation not ..." (2 Corinthians 7:10, KJV). Third, the person's will must respond to God in receiving Christ (see John 1:12), repentance (see Acts 3:36), and yielding himself unto God (see Romans 6:13). Saving faith is both passive and active, according to Augustus Hopkins Strong. In his standard theology text he writes:

> We need to emphasize this active element in saving faith, lest men get the notion that mere indolent acquiescence in Christ's plan will save them. Faith is not simple receptiveness. It gives itself, as well as receives Christ. It is not mere passivity—it is also self-committal. As all reception of knowledge is active, and there must be attention if we would learn, so all reception of Christ is active, and there must be intelligent giving as well as taking.[2]

3. *Justifying faith*. Paul uses an unusual expression, "being justified by faith," primarily in the book of Romans to reveal how God justifies or "declares us righteous" because of our faith. The phrase "being justified by faith" (Romans 5:1) means that out of a person's faith, God declares the record of the believer perfect in Heaven. The believer is not made perfect, because he still has a sinful nature and will not stop sinning until he arrives in Heaven. God stamps perfection on the believer's record when he is saved/converted. This is a non-experiential action that is not

felt in the believer's daily life. But when the believer realizes the truth of justifying faith, he should respond by changing his lifestyle. According to Martyn Lloyd-Jones, being justified by faith "does three things for us at once. It gives us peace with God; it puts us firmly in the place of all blessings; and it enables us to exult at the prospect of our future final glorification." While there is no inherent power or experience in justifying faith, it becomes the basis of the next type of faith.

4. *Indwelling faith.* Jesus challenged His disciples to have greater faith. He offered them the power to cast mountains into the sea when He declared, "Have the faith of God" (see Mark 11:22-23). While the King James Version translates it "have faith in God," the original is *pisteuo theuo*, genitive, which is "have God's faith." This indwelling faith gives the believer the power of God to solve problems or remove barriers (mountains) in his life. Sometimes this is called the deeper-life faith, for it gives the believer power beyond himself.

Despite his reputation as a great man of faith, George Mueller denied he had the gift of faith but rather explained that his faith was "the self-same faith which is found in every believer, and the growth of which I am most sensible of to myself; for by little and little it has been increasing for the last sixty-nine years.[3]

The power of indwelling faith is gained by yielding a problem to God, following biblical principles in solving the problem, expressing faith in God's solution, not doubting, and praying for a solution. Then the believer must act on what he/she knows. This action is the result of indwelling faith.

The experience of indwelling faith grows as the believer trusts God for greater things. However, there is no perfection in any human, so not everything the deeper-life believer claims will come about, and not everything the great men of faith, like Falwell and Mueller, say will actually happen. Nevertheless, those who experience deeper-life faith know that they are walking with God and are assured that God will operate through them in the future because He had done it in the past. Those who experience deeper-life faith are keenly aware that: There is no power in themselves, they are evidently human, their strength is in the Bible, but their fellowship with Christ is real.

5. *Living by faith.* The Bible admonishes, "the just shall live by faith" (Romans 1:17; Habakkuk 2:4; Galatians 3:11; Hebrews 10:38). To this command, Paul adds, "For we walk by faith, not by sight" (2 Corinthians 5:7). This book uses the phrase "faith-walking." The experience and testimony of some faith missions' boards and faith Bible institutes lead certain people interpret living by faith as trusting God for money. What they did was exercise indwelling faith, let Christ's faith answer their needs. They may exercise the spiritual gift of faith to solve their money problems, but this is a very limited view of living by faith. It is more than trusting God for money; it is trusting Him for everything ... every need in life.

The experience of living by faith is simply living by the principles of Scripture (the faith). As one writer expressed his view of the importance of living by faith:

> Faith, I realized, isn't just another of the good activities in the Christian life. It is the basis—the one essential—for hearing God's "Well done!" God had been trying to tell me through all those faith experiences that Christian activity was good, but the one thing He wanted me to do was to trust Him. Faith in Christ isn't just an additive for an extra-good Christian life—it is the Christian life.[4]

Technically speaking, living by faith doesn't give the believer power to live the deeper Christian life, nor does it give him the experience of fellowship with God. But when he orders his life by the principles of

Scripture, he has a basis for the experience of the deeper Christian life and a basis for getting things by faith from God.

Since there are different levels of knowing Scripture, there are different levels of living by faith. The new Christian can immediately begin to live by faith, no matter how elementary his life or his conversion. The mature believer who has controlled his life by Scripture can also continue to grow in faith. Living by faith is a cognitive experience that is the objective basis for an inner deeper-life experience.

6. *The spiritual gift of faith*. The ultimate expression of faith is an ability to solve problems or move mountains by faith. The spiritual gift of faith is called a spiritual gift, also called a spiritual ability (see Romans 12:3,6; 1 Corinthians 12:9; 13:2). It is given to some and not all Christians (see 1 Corinthians 12:11), as are all spiritual gifts. It seems to be greater in some than in others. But like all spiritual gifts, we can seek it (see 1 Corinthians 12:31), and it can grow in its manifestation. Donald Gee defines this spiritual gift, noting:

> The spiritual gift of faith is a special quality of faith, sometimes called by our older theologians the "faith of miracles." It would seem to come upon certain of God's servants in times of special crisis or opportunity in such mighty power that they are lifted right out of the realm of even natural and ordinary faith in God—and have a divine certainty put within their soul that triumphs over everything. It is a magnificent gift and is probably exercised frequently with far-reaching results.[5]

The spiritual gift of faith is an experience of complete trust in God for His blessing in their Christian service. Those who experience this ability probably have met the criteria of the previous five categories of faith. The spiritual gift of faith in a person will grow with his knowledge of Scripture, with his awareness of his new position before God, with his experience of the deeper life of indwelling faith, and with his application of the principles of Scripture to his life.

DEFINITION OF FAITH

The noun "faith" is *pistis* in the Greek language. In the perfect tense, it is a non-verb hybrid, "to have belief." The verb *pisteuo* is an action word, i.e., believe, trust, rely on, act on, receive, accept, or rest on. The object of your faith must motivate or activate you to respond, either outwardly or inwardly.

Therefore, faith is validated by the authenticity of its object, i.e., the thing, action, or the person into which you are placing your faith. Therefore, when you put your faith in God, you get God's action and God's response. When you put your faith in business, you only get the response of the power of that business. Do you put your faith in your church, or in anything else?

Therefore, it is not your faith that heals; it is God who does the healing. It is not faith that sends millions of dollars to those who ask for it; it is God. So, when you say faith, make sure you understand your faith is in God, who is the object of your faith. Without God your faith is nothing.

Faith is a road that God uses to get you where you are going. Faith is a tool that God uses to fix your problem. Faith is the medicine that God uses to heal. So look beyond your faith and look to God, who uses your faith to change things.

What is faith? The Bible explains and defines faith: "Now faith is the substance of things hoped for, the evidence of things not seen" (Hebrews 11:1). Let's take the old King James and put it into modern terminology: "Faith is the title deed that gives you ownership of things hoped for; faith is the inner conviction that your answer exists" (Hebrews 11:1, ELT).

FAITH HAS MANY SIZES

Mountain-moving faith. Faith can move a mountain, i.e., a financial mountain, a spiritual mountain, even personal barriers. Didn't Jesus say, "Have faith in God. I tell you the truth, you can say to this mountain, may you be lifted up and thrown into the sea, and it will happen. But you must really believe that it will happen and have not doubt in your heart" (Mark 11:22-23, NLT)? Jerry Falwell and Liberty University are evidence God honors mountain-moving faith.

Great faith. There are many people who trust God for small things. Jesus recognized this when He asked the question "Why do you have so little faith?" (Matthew 6:30).

Some giants in the Old Testament began with weak faith, as did Abraham: "Abraham ... who against hope ... weak faith" (Romans 4:16,18-19). He may have begun with weak faith, but later it was said of Abraham, "... did not waver at the promise of God ... but was strengthened in faith" (Romans 4:20).

If you have weak faith, it can grow in strength. If you have strong faith, it can grow even stronger. The disciples had faith in the physical Jesus, yet they wanted more faith; they prayed, "Lord, increase our faith" (Luke 17:5).

NOTES

1. James I. Packer, "Faith," Baker's Dictionary of Theology, ed. Everett F. Harrison (Grand Rapids, MI: Baker Book House, 1960), 209.

2. Augustus Hopkins Strong, *Systematic Theology* (Old Tappan, NJ: Fleming H. Revell Co., 1907), 838.

3. George Mueller, *Autobiography of George Mueller* (London: J. Nisbet & Co., 1905), 173.

4. Russ Johnston with Maureen Rank, *God Can Make It Happen* (Wheaton, IL: Victor Books, 1977), 7.

5. Donald Gee, *Concerning Spiritual Gifts* (Springfield, MO: Gospel Publishing House, 1972), 42.

Chapter 3

A LEAP OF FAITH

WHAT is a leap? A dictionary defines "leap" as "to spring free, as from the ground; to jump over a fence; to pass abruptly from one state to another; to act precipitately."

Usually, a leap is stepping over an obstacle or barrier, and involves being suspended in the air while moving from one place to another. But the most important aspect of a leap is its destination. Where are you going? Where will you be when you land?

Did Jesus intend to include a leap of faith when He said, "Whosoever says to this mountain, 'be removed and cast into the sea,' and does not doubt in his heart, but believes ... he will have whatever he says" (Mark 11:23)? Is moving a mountain a leap of faith?

While Jesus did not actually mean to take a physical leap, He does tell us to make bold, aggressive decisions and act on our decisions to get what we want/need from God.

Abraham's faith stepped over his inner obstacles to follow God and get what he wanted from God. "And being not weak in faith ... he staggered not at the promises of God" (Romans 4:19-20). God had said to Abraham, "Get out of your country ... and from your father's house to

---

a land that I will show you" (Genesis 12:1). Obviously, Abraham had to move from one place to another; was that a step of faith ... a bold leap of faith?

God only promised Abraham, "to a land that I will show you" (Genesis 12:1). Thus far God had not promised to give him the land, only to show it to him. Abraham took a leap/step of faith to see what God had for him.

Remember, your faith in God is based on a relationship with Him. "But without faith it is impossible to please Him, for he who comes to God must believe that He is, and that He is a rewarder of those who diligently seek Him" (Hebrews 11:6). Two things about this verse: first, it involves those who are "coming to God," and second, "those who diligently or continually seek Him." While this verse does not describe a leap of faith, it does describe the idea of making a bold step from where you are to where God is calling you to leap.

Jerry Falwell once said, "Faith is stepping out into the darkness, into the unknown." This is what Abraham did: "But Abraham ... went out, not knowing where he was going" (Hebrews 11:8). Abraham exercised faith in his obedience. What kind of faith? The author of Hebrews said, "faith is ... the evidence of things not seen" (Hebrews 11:1). Abraham's obedience resulted in going where he had not yet seen.

Is faith a leap into the dark? Notice what God promised Noah. Noah spent years building the ark. Why? "Noah ... divinely warned of things not yet seen" (Hebrews 11:7). It had never rained or flooded the earth. Yet God told Noah a flood was coming. Noah believed God and acted on information about a flood he had not seen and not experienced. That was an act of faith.

So, what is faith? Faith is obedience to the call/word of God. "Abraham obeyed when he was called" (Hebrews 11:9). So, when you take a step of faith, you are obeying the word of God, and when God leads you, you are obeying the leading of God. This is faith.

Faith is claiming a promise. Sarah, wife to Abraham, was part of his faith journey. She had not had a child, yet God promised she was going to have a child. When God promised she was going to have a son, "Sarah ... judged Him faithful who had promised" (Hebrews 11:11). Faith is acting on the word of God. Both Sarah and Abraham acted on what God told them to do. "Abraham ... offered up Isaac ... who had received the promise" (Hebrews 11:17). The greatest act of faith in the life of Abraham was his willingness to offer his son Isaac on the altar to God.

Just as quickly as we describe faith as obedience, also faith is claiming a promise, and faith is acting quickly and obediently. Some have acted in faith but did not realize what they sought from God in their lifetime. "These all died in faith, not having received the promise" (Hebrews 11:13). The author of Hebrews tells of people who responded in faith and did what God told them to do but did not receive the promise that they expected in their lifetime. Rather, they died in faith.

Some took steps of faith but did not get physical freedom, but rather, "By faith ... were tortured, not accepting deliverance" (Hebrews 11:31,35). "By faith ... still others had trial of mockings and scourgings, yes, and of chains and imprisonment" (Hebrews 11:31,36). God had a different purpose for them.

If you act in obedience to God but do not receive what you wanted, think of Paul, who had "a thorn in the flesh" (2 Corinthians 12:7). Paul prayed three times for God's deliverance, yet he never received deliverance. Rather, Paul said, "I pleaded with the Lord three times that it might depart from me" (2 Corinthians 12:8). Paul asked for healing but never received it in his lifetime, yet he lived in faith.

PREPARING TO LEAP

When you talk about taking a step of faith, or a leap of faith, what must you do to prepare yourself for that experience? First, make sure you are right in your planning. Also, you want to make sure you are right in what you expect to receive. How can you prepare?

1. Ask if you really want to take this leap.

Sometimes you want to take a leap, but ask yourself, *Is this leap rally for me, or is it for God?* You have to ask yourself, is this really a leap of faith or is this a leap of your self-desire or self-perception? You must realistically face this question before you take this leap of faith.

2. The higher or longer the leap, the more energy will be needed to reach the destination.

Sometimes your leap involves more time in planning so that you pray longer and harder about it. Sometimes the bigger the leap, the more you must plan your preparation and actions. But more does not always mean more time. It could mean more people praying with you, and praying more intensely on their part, as well as yours.

This includes more planning and more preparation on your part. But also, as you think about how big and long your leap will be, think in terms of support from others, such as your family, fellow workers, and those who are following you. Are they going to have to take the same leap at a later time, or will they take the leap with you?

Remember, make sure you are leaping properly, because you cannot change strategies when you are in the air; you cannot change your destination when you are halfway there.

3. Consider where you will land and where you will be after you take the leap.

Sometimes you have to look at what your leap accomplishes, and ask yourself if you really want it. It is not just a successful landing you need; ask if you are landing where you have aimed. Do you really want what you are asking God to give you? Beyond what you want, do you really need it?

Then another question: what will you do when you get there? Once you get victory, how will you live for God? What will you do to serve God? How can you accomplish more for God?

4. Don't spend so much energy in your leap that you cannot live or minister when you get to your destination.

Sometimes people spend all of their time and energy planning for money and resources to get ready to leap. And when they leap and arrive, they have no energy to live, or minister, or do the work of God that motivated them to leap in the first place.

5. Some leaps must be taken in spite of fear and obstacles.

When you think in terms of taking a great leap/step of faith, sometimes your fears will be so great that you cannot move. But you must take that step because God's work necessitates advancement. The victory you need is absolutely necessary to keep the work of God going forward. So you have to make the leap, because the work of God will not go forward without it.

But then think about the reputation of God. When you take a leap of faith, you not only put yourself on the spot, but also you put God on the spot. You said that God will supply your needs, but what if the needs are not supplied? Have you made a mistake? Should you have leaped in the first place?

One last question: Is the leap imperative for you personally? Do you take a leap for your own self-esteem, or for your own growth/progress, or for the work of God?

6. Some leaps are so dangerous, you might not survive.

So, before you take a leap of faith, ask yourself some questions: What will happen to the work of God if the leap is not successful? Will the work of God be hurt? Can the work be carried on that God originally called you to do?

Another question: what will happen to the people with you if the leap is unsuccessful? What happens to them? To your family? To your fellow workers? To those running the race beside you? What will happen to the work of God if the leap is not successful?

Finally, ask yourself the question, what will happen to you if you fail after making this dangerous leap? What will happen to your work in the world?

RESULTS OF THE LEAP OF FAITH

1. You have intimacy.

When you take a leap of faith for God, you not only are moving the work of God forward, but you are moving yourself closer to the heart of God. "Enoch walked with God, and he was not, for God took him" (Genesis 5:24). When Enoch took that faith step, he got closer to God, so close that God took him to Heaven without dying. When you take your leap of faith, will you have closer fellowship with God? Will you be more intimate with God than ever before? Will you be ready to do more for God than ever before?

2. The work is accomplished.

You take a leap of faith to accomplish a work of God. Notice what happened to Noah: "By faith Noah ... prepared an ark" (Hebrews 11:7). Noah's leap of faith was to spend multiple years building an ark. He had to work in spite of the laughter of those who mocked him. He did it because God had told him what to do. We wonder in the secrets of the dark night if Noah ever doubted if he was doing the right thing. But at the same time, God had spoken to him, and Noah heard the voice of God. What else could he do but obey?

3. You leave security.

As you take a leap and are flying in the middle of the air, you have nothing secure under your feet. Where are you? Are you in the arms of God? Are you walking on the promise of God? Are you claiming the protection of God? "By faith Abraham ... went out not knowing where he was going" (Hebrews 11:8). Abraham was 50 years old when God called him to go to the Promised Land and promised to use him to begin a nation for God. He was 99 years old when Sarah conceived the son God had promised. That is a long time to wait, and that is a long time to continue trusting God.

4. You involve others.

Not only does your faith involve you and your future, but it also involves others and their future. Notice that Isaac's faith involved his sons: "By faith Isaac blessed" (Hebrews 11:20) his sons, Esau and Jacob, to give them the promise of God for their lives and futures. Isaac's faith drew his sons into a faith relationship with him and with God. Why? Because they were going to receive what God had promised and be a part of living what God would do.

5. Faith beyond this life.

Sometimes your leap of faith involves your life and circumstances beyond the grave. Joseph made a faith statement concerning where he should be buried: "By faith Joseph ... gave instructions concerning his bones" (Hebrews 11:22). It was a faith statement when he told his family to take his bones back to the Promised Land and bury them there.

6. Faith involves immediate experiences.

Moses chose to follow God and at the same time he turned his back on his heritage and future in Pharaoh's palace. He had been raised by Pharaoh's daughter, trained to be a Pharaoh one day, but he left it all when he chose to follow God. "By faith Moses ... choosing ... to suffer affliction" (Hebrews 11:25).

7. Faith involves others.

Sometimes your leap of faith will involve others. You have to ask, what will happen to them? What consequences will they suffer? What rewards will they enjoy? When Rahab received the spies into her house and protected them, she took a leap of faith. When she sent them out and didn't tell the authorities about them, again it was a leap/step of faith. "By faith Rahab ... received the spies in peace" (Hebrews 11:31).

8. A step of faith to accomplish a goal.

Look at young 16-year-old David, a keeper of his father's sheep. He went to visit his brother at the camp where the Philistines and Israelites were lined up in battle. Then Goliath came out to curse the people of God and threaten them, but more than that, he challenged them to a battle. David took the leap of faith to defend the honor of God, the honor of the nation, and his own family: "By faith ... David" (Hebrews 11:31-32).

SUMMARY

As you read about the people in Scripture who made a leap of faith, ask yourself, *Will I ever have to a make a leap of faith?* Or, *When will I make my leap of faith?* Don't ask if you will be successful or if you will fail. That is a question of doubt. Ask if you will obey.

Your first leap/step of faith may be a baby step. You don't remember your first step, but at some time, and in some circumstance, you did it. You don't remember if someone helped you, or if you were alone, and just let go to take a step. It wasn't awesome to the world, but your first step was important to you—it meant you could do it. You did what all others have done. You started something you would do in your lifetime. You walked!

The same way with your first step of faith for God. It may not have been awesome to others, but it marked a beginning for you. It may have been a baby step, but it started you on a life of faith. It started you faith-walking. Isn't that what this book is all about? If you have ever taken your first baby step of faith, then you did it. You *faith*-walked! Now keep doing it. Walking stronger—walking faster—walking longer—faith-walking to serve and glorify God.

Chapter 4

IT TAKES TWO
WINGS TO FLY

G OD created birds to fly, and He gave them two wings to do it. A one-winged bird cannot fly, because it does not have balance ... lift ... nor energy and speed. It takes two wings to fly!

For a bird to get off the ground, it must have both wings. If it only has one wing, it will not leave the ground, and if it loses one wing while flying, it will crash.

To help birds fly, God follows the law of balance and lift. It is the same law God applies to our salvation.

The first wing is faith, i.e., *saving faith*, which is belief in the Lord Jesus Christ. "Believe the Lord Jesus Christ and you will be saved" (Acts 16:31). The second wing is *daily faith*. Paul challenges us to "walk by faith" (2 Corinthians 5:7).

The first wing of *saving faith* is when you turn to God from the old life of sin; you turn away from the evil that will destroy you in hell if you had not turned to God. Paul notes of the Thessalonians, "You turned to God from idols" (1 Thessalonians 1: 9).

Turning involves two actions. First you turn from where you were facing, or where you were going. Second, you turn to your new destination, or your new vision of the future. In salvation you turn from sin to Jesus Christ. Why? Because Jesus died for your sins. He gave His life to forgive your sin; therefore, you must do everything to find the way to Heaven—to find salvation.

You can't be saved by repentance alone.

You can't be saved without repentance.

Peter preached repentance (see Acts 2:38), and so did Paul (see Acts 17:20,26). So the first wing is turning from sin and turning to God. The first is the salvation wing. Then the second wing is daily or continually living or walking by faith. "We walk by faith, not by sight" (2 Corinthians 5:7). This second wing is faith-walking, looking only to God, and trusting in His Word.

Let's look at faith-walking. Faith-walking is your continuing relationship with God. James explains how we faith-walk.

FAITH AND WORKS APPLIED TO WALKING

"How effectively can the Christian fly who has one wing of faith but not the natural wing of human effort? Can his faith wing make him fly? If the [one-winged believer] sees a needy Christian and only blesses him in faith, has he done any good? No, his Christian friend is still needy. So a believer with only a faith wing, without a practical wing, can't fly. A believer can't say, 'I have [faith Christianity] but you only have [practical Christianity]. If they first tried to show faith without practical actions, they will not get off the ground. If you have only a faith wing and believe in God, what good is that? The demons also believe in one God, but they at least tremble. You are dumb if you think faith without being practical will work. As the body without the spirit is dead, so your faith is dead if it doesn't have both faith and practical application" (James 2:14-20,26, ELT).

FAITH-WALKING AND WORKS

Just as a bird with one wing will never get off the ground, so too the Christian who only has faith without works will never live for God, nor please God. "Without faith it is impossible to please Him, for he who comes to God must believe that He is, and that He is a rewarder of those who diligently seek Him" (Hebrews 11:6).

Your works are empty without faith. No matter how hard you work, you can never please God, because you are a sinner. You were born in sin and never reach perfection. "Faith without works is dead" (v. 17).

Your faith will not fly without works. The passage from James teaches us very clearly that your faith is dead if faith doesn't live in your daily ministry. "Can't you see that faith without good deeds is useless?" (James 2:20, NLT).

Why both faith and works. Because it takes faith to reach God and it takes works to manifest that your faith is authentic and represents an honest dependence upon God.

Faith that flies must have God's life, God's presence, and God's blessing. When you have faith, it is more than belief; your faith attaches to God, and He gives life to you and to your works/service. And how do you live that life? You believe and obey the Scriptures; you pray; you walk and live to please Him.

You pray for God to supply money to live, then you work hard for a raise, promotion, or commission. In the Old Testament the Jews were promised financial prosperity when they lived in the land of promise, but they had to work hard to obtain that prosperity. At the same time, they had to trust God as they brought their yearly sacrifices to Him and paid tithes and offerings. You must have the same commitment with your faith in God alone, but also show works by the way you serve Christ ... the way you witness for Christ ... and the way you offer financial gifts to Him.

You pray best for conversions as you share the gospel with unsaved people. Usually, the more people to whom you witness, the more who are likely to get saved. So you must invite people to hear the gospel, either from the pulpit or you must explain it to them—add to this evangelistic church visitation. The church with the greatest visitation program usually has the best harvest in souls reached for Jesus Christ.

You pray best for church growth when you do the things that make your church grow. You must visit the lost and invite them to church. The church must advertise evangelistic meetings and tell what God is doing. Your church must plan for visitors, and when they come, make sure they are welcomed into church fellowship. If you want new members to come to your church, you must go and bring the unsaved into the church, as well as people who are saved but have no church home.

You cannot pray for church attendance to grow if your church has not provided parking, pews, programs for growth.

HOW FAITH AND WORKS
COME TOGETHER

Start by committing yourself to practical ministry. There are challenges and opportunities where you can pray for God to work, trust

Him for results, and by faith see God working in others as well as in yourself. But the key is faith. You must believe God for results, and when your faith works in relationship to God, He works.

Perhaps you will take a leap of faith to let God work when you face a challenge or obstacle or burden. A problem or challenge may have slowed you down or stopped you, but pray, trust God, and take a leap of faith by asking God to open doors to give victory. But also notice, the leap of faith is based on daily ministry ... daily work ... daily faithfulness. When you add faith and works together, you find God's faithfulness will work through your ministry.

If you begin by faith, make sure that you continue in faith. Sometimes you might take a leap of faith, where God answers in a great way, but after a while when the work progresses, you begin to rely more on your works than faith. Be careful! Faith and works always work together ... always.

One without the other will never work. It will not work if you depend on God to do half the work while you do the other half of the work. Remember, we are in partnership with God. We work together with Him. Both you and God work at the same time. "We are workmen together with God" (1 Corinthians 3:9). That does not mean you do the first half and let God finish the second half. You cannot divide up spiritual work like that. Both you and God work at the same time ... you both begin together and work together all the time ... till the project is done.

Division of labor. This is the law that describes how we accomplish things for God. You work as though everything depends on you. Then you trust God to work as though everything depends on Him. That means both you and God are fully dependent all of the time, for all the work, and for all the results.

Both faith and works begin with a burden. Sometimes God gives a deep desire or passion for His work; this is also called a burden. And what is a burden like? When you pick up a heavy stone that you cannot carry, it is a burden you must either put down or get help to carry. Sometimes you pick up the work of God, which may be a Sunday school class or it might be something larger, like the weight of a church. A burden can even be a private problem. But a burden is heavy ... physically draining ... and mentally challenging. And what do you do with a burden? You apply both faith and works together at the same time ... every time ... all the time.

What works best? Obviously works by itself is not best, nor is it enough. It takes faith and works together ... partnering together ... ministering together ... trusting together ... following Jesus Christ together.

So, what kind of prayer is effective? When you see and find His presence so that you are ministering with the presence of Jesus Christ, you are able to accomplish more in ministry.

So, when you pray, seek God's will and guidance. He has a plan for your personal life, and God has a plan for everything that you do. Therefore, find God's purpose and do it to fulfill His glory.

Chapter 5

FAITH TO USE SPIRITUAL GIFTS

Desire earnestly the best gifts.

1 Corinthians 12:31

THE Bible exhorts us to desire the best gifts. Do you have that wonderful and logical desire, but the question remains, how can you find which are your best spiritual gifts? And when you find out what they are, how can you put those spiritual gifts to work? Does knowing/finding your best spiritual gifts automatically mean you will use them, or can you even know how to use them?

Today God is still giving spiritual gifts to His followers. That means He is giving spiritual gifts to you. These gifts are part of the tools He has provided to help you accomplish your part in the task of world evangelization. Also, they are given for your ministry with other Christians; that way you can help build up the body of Christ. They fall into two categories: enabling gifts and task gifts.

First, enabling gifts. Among the gifts that are operative for today are the enabling gifts that all Christians seem to possess. This is more than the gift of salvation (see Romans 5:15-16; 6:23); these are general enabling abilities that are given to help each Christian live for Christ and serve Christ: (1) faith (see Romans 1:11; 1 Corinthians 12:9), (2) knowledge (see 1 Corinthians 12:8), (3) wisdom (see 1 Corinthians 12:8), and (4) discernment (see 1 Corinthians 12:10). These general gifts help the believer use their specific task gifts.

Second, task gifts. These are special abilities that are given by the Holy Spirit for you, the believer, to serve God. Not every believer has each of these task gifts, and not every believer possessing each task gift has the same level of effectiveness. The following chart will help distinguish between spiritual gifts.

THE GIFTS OF THE SPIRIT

Sign Gifts

(no longer available)

1. Apostle,
   Ephesians 4:11

2. Healing,
   1 Corinthians 12:9

3. Tongues,
   1 Corinthians 12:10

4. Interpretation of tongues,
   1 Corinthians 12:10

Serving Gifts

Enabling Gifts for All
Believers Today

1. Faith,
   1 Corinthians 12:9

2. Knowledge,
   1 Corinthians 12:8

3. Wisdom,
   1 Corinthians 12:8

4. Discernment,
   1 Corinthians 12:10

Task Gifts
for Specific Believers Today

1. Prophecy, Romans 12:6

2. Teaching, Romans 12:7

3. Exhortation, Romans 12:8

4. Shepherding (pastoring),
   Ephesians 4:11

5. Showing mercy, 1 Corinthians 12:8

6. Ministering, Romans 12:7

7. Helps, 1 Corinthians 12:28

8. Giving, Romans 12:8

9. Ruling, Romans 12:8

10. Governments, 1 Corinthians 12:28

11. Evangelists (church planting), Ephesians 4:11

12. Hospitality, 1 Peter 4:9

13. Prophecy, Romans 12:6

Our primary attention is to the serving gift, also called the spiritual gift of faith. This gift of faith is given to all believers to help them use/activate a specific ability/spiritual gift. As an illustration, a person can have both a natural and a spiritual ability to teach, but when that person uses their spiritual gift of faith as they are instructing, it will be more effective. How much more effective? The stronger the person's spiritual gift of faith, the more results will flow from his teaching.

When Paul described spiritual gifts in Romans 12:3-8, he first listed the spiritual gift of faith (a serving gift). Paul begins telling us, "not to think more highly than he ought to think, but to think soberly as God has dealt to each one a measure of faith" (Romans 12:3). Then Paul tells how "having these gifts differing ... let us use them, if prophecy ... or ministering ... or teaching ... or exhortation ... or giving [money] ... or showing mercy" (Romans 12:6-8). Because faith is mentioned first before all other spiritual abilities/gifts, we conclude that you should use your spiritual gift of faith as you exercise/employ your other spiritual gifts.

MANY PURPOSES OF FAITH

We have previously shown that there is more than one expression of faith, i.e., "from faith to faith" (Romans 1:17). That suggests that you can have various intensities of faith. That is evident because the Bible describes some with weak faith (see Romans 14:1) and others with strong faith (see Romans 4:20). Also, there are varieties of faith, e.g., faith to accomplish certain tasks (saving faith, living by faith, justifying faith, indwelling faith, and the topic of this chapter, the spiritual gift of faith).

Remember, sometimes faith is not strong enough (see Romans 14:1) and at other times it is not the strength of faith but simply the presence of faith as opposed to lack of faith (see Matthew 14:11). That leads us to getting more faith, or growing our faith stronger.

We learn that our faith can grow in strength as we add to the number of our spiritual gifts from this exhortation by Paul: "Desire earnestly the best gifts" (1 Corinthians 12:31).

But beyond our many spiritual gifts, Paul tells us we have an identifying spiritual gift: "Everyone has his proper gift" (1 Corinthians 7:7). This "proper gift" seems to be our strength, or the dominant ability by which we are identified. The phrase "proper gift" (v. 7, KJV) is also translated "special gift" (v. 7, TEV), "his own gift from God" (v. 7, NIV), "his own particular gift" (v. 7, Phillips), "his special gift" (v. 7, RSV), and "the gift God has granted" (v. 7, NEB). This does not seem to be "the spiritual gift" of faith but a specific-task spiritual gift.

The Bible teaches that the believer has all spiritual gifts embryonically. That means you may have the potential of serving God with a spiritual gift you don't know about because that gift has not been found, or it has not manifested itself as you serve God.

Why do you have all spiritual gifts embryonically? Because you have the Holy Spirit indwelling you, and He is the source of all spiritual gifts. The Holy Spirit came into your life when you were converted (see 1 Corinthians 3:16; 2 Corinthians 6:15-18). Also, the Bible teaches and expects all believers to do/perform all spiritual ministries. You could not do what God expects you to do if you did not have the enablement of the Holy Spirit, who works in you by the gifts He gives you.

Therefore, we are to use our gift of faith "having then different expressions of faith" (Romans 12:3, ELT); let us use our faith to express all our spiritual gifts.

THE TASK OF FAITH

There are several tasks manifested in Scripture that are linked to faith. Let's look at each of these to see how faith works with each spiritual gift.

1. Evangelism faith is simple obedience to God's command.

When Christ gave the Great Commission, it was specific: "Go therefore and make disciples of all the nations, baptizing them in the name of the Father and of the Son and of the Holy Spirit" (Matthew 28:19). While that is a command to the church, it also applies to individuals. Each individual Christian has an obligation to evangelize through their local church to reach lost people with the gospel.

2. Serving/ministering

Use your faith when ushering, serving in a church office, or ministering to individuals. It takes faith to see God at work in others.

3. Counseling/mercy showing

Remember, "God has dealt to each one a measure of faith ... He that showeth mercy" (Romans 12:3,8, KJV). It takes faith to see God working in the lives of others; and as you share the Word of God with them, also share practical lessons God the Holy Spirit has taught you. Your gift of faith can apply the message to the life of those you are helping.

4. Teaching/Christian explanation

"God has dealt the measure of faith ... on teaching" (Romans 12:3,7). This fits with the other explanation by Paul: "and He gave some ... teachers" (Ephesians 4:11). Those with the gift of teaching also are given by

God a passion to share and learn the Word of God. Paul ties the spiritual gift of faith to the spiritual gift of teaching: "Though I have the gift ... and understand all knowledge and mysteries and though I have all faith" (1 Corinthians 13:2). Here Paul uses faith to both know the Scriptures and then to share it with others. Therefore, if you will be a teacher for God, pray that He will use your spiritual gift of faith to help you learn the Word of God better and deeper, and then share it both theologically and practically.

5. Exhortation, or encouragement

This is the spiritual gift to motivate people to overcome difficulties and problems so they can live for God. Therefore, "God hath dealt ... the measure of faith ... he that exhorteth" (Romans 12:3,6, KJV). Exhortation involves both knowing what we must say to others (your content) and how to say it (your method of communication).

6. Prophecy/correction/warning/rebuke and preaching

This spiritual gift is much more than the typical definition given by many, that it deals with prediction(s) about the future or future events. When examining the word "prophecy," it deals with speaking the word of God to people to direct their lives, connect their actions, or help them in their faith. This is what Paul meant when he said, "Let us prophesy according to the proportion of faith" (Romans 6:3,6). Those who prophecy have a deep commitment to the person and nature of God. They want people to know God properly, so they obey Him explicitly, and serve Him with all their energy.

7. Shepherding/pastoring/leading

This spiritual gift includes pastors and teachers in our churches and Christian institutions that support the church and the Great Commission. But shepherding also includes the "pastoring role" done by lay people. As an illustration, a Sunday school teacher is the extension of the pastor, who is responsible to teach the Word of God to the whole church. A Sunday school teacher will be delegated to their class to carry out that teaching responsibly. "And He gave some ... pastors and teachers" (Ephesians 4:11).

8. Administration/managing/directing

This spiritual gift is the task of those who are responsible for the organization and administration of the local church. They use their spiritual gift of administration for the work of the ministry through their church. "God hath dealt the measure of faith ... he that ruleth" (Romans 12:3,8, KJV) and governments (see 1 Corinthians 12:28). Those with the serving gift of administration and the overseeing gift of faith will be used by God to place the right believers in the right place, at the right time, to do the right job in the right way.

9. Giving/supporting

This spiritual gift of giving is usually associated with giving money to the church. That is its primary meaning, but it also includes a "giving attitude" so that the believer will give their time, talent, and treasure to God. When using the spiritual gift of faith with donations of money, it will accomplish God's purpose in a better way. "God hath dealt the measure of faith ... he that giveth" (Romans 12:3,8).

10. Overcoming obstacles, problems, situations

The Bible describes this spiritual gift as the ability to eliminate obstacles that hinder the work of God. "Though I have all faith ... to remove mountains [barriers]" (1 Corinthians 13:2). Paul is describing love in the above chapter and he explains the greatness of love by associating it with the gift of faith to overcome obstacles. Why here? Because faith is foundational to Christian belief and action, as is love. To Paul, faith and love go together. Paul was building on the principle given by Jesus: "If you have faith as a grain of mustard seed, you will say to this mountain, 'move' ... it shall move" (Matthew 17:20).

11. Dealing with pain/suffering/affliction

The Bible tells you to glorify God when you endure pain by faith, because your faith will help you endure suffering. Peter writes about "the trial of your faith" (1 Peter 1:7). James also mentions the same idea: "The trying of your faith" (James 1:3). Both of these men understood trials and persecution, so they tie faith to trials to give it additional meaning.

Chapter 6

THINGS THAT HINDER/WEAKEN FAITH

FAITH is a relationship with God, and that relationship can be weak (see Romans 4:19) or it can grow strong (see Romans 4:20). We are challenged not to have weak faith. Remember that Jesus said to Peter, "O you of little faith" (Matthew 14:31). Again Jesus challenged, "be not faithless" (John 20:27).

So, is it possible for a believer to have weak faith or little faith? This chapter will analyze why some Christians have weak/little faith. If you have weak or little faith, pray like the father who asked Jesus, "Lord ... help my unbelief" (Mark 9:24).

21 THINGS THAT WEAKEN FAITH

Since faith is a reflection of your relationship with God, then anything that weakens that relationship also weakens your faith. First, just thinking about sin will surely weaken your faith. This could be thinking about doing something that we know is wrong and will weaken our faith. But we don't need to think about doing it, or getting its results for ourselves, or any other way to benefit from sin; we can just think about sin or we dream or desire to sin, and that will weaken our faith. The psalmist wrote, "If I regard iniquity in my heart ..." (Psalm 66:18). "Regard" means just sin thinking, or sin day dreaming, or sin planning. What will happen when we open the door to sin thinking? "The Lord will not hear me" (Psalm 66:18).

A second thing to weaken faith is your ignorance of Scripture. If you don't know the Scriptures, you will have weak faith. "Faith comes by hearing ... the Word of God" (Romans 10:13). The old adage says, "Little Scripture knowledge leads to little faith, or more Scripture knowledge leads to bigger faith." This thinking that weakens our faith could be called "the sin of ignorance." Because we won't take the time/energy to study/learn the Bible, we don't grow in faith. What will weaken your faith? Just doing nothing with the Bible. You don't study ... learn ... and apply it to daily life. Why is that called a sin? Because we are exhorted/commanded to hear the Bible (see Revelation 1:3), read/study the Bible (see 2 Timothy 2:15), meditate/think on the Bible (see Joshua 1:8), and obey it (see 1 Peter 1:22). Therefore, we ought to be aggressively learning the Bible and applying it to our daily lives.

The third thing that will weaken your faith is when you stop applying your faith to your daily life. What you know or learn in the Scriptures, you don't apply to your daily life. This lets our faith slowly die. James describes this condition as "faith is dead" (James 2:7).

The fourth thing that will weaken your faith is wrong motives. We don't apply ourselves to the demands of faith. James tells us that when we spend our time satisfying our desires or pleasures, our prayers won't be answered. "You receive not ... because you spend it upon your pleasures" (James 4:3).

The Bible identifies our problem as "the lust of the eyes, the lust of the flesh, and the pride of life" (1 John 2:15-17). At the very core of the lust and pride is the "I" factor, or the "self" factor. We must lean and apply "not I but Christ" (Galatians 2:20). When we say no to our selfish agenda and say yes to God's priorities, we begin to strengthen our faith and grow our faith.

The fifth thing that will weaken your faith is simply doing nothing about your faith. There are those who simply do nothing to grow in Christ. These are those who do not give time to learning the Scriptures or sharing the Scriptures with others, with friends, family, and co-workers. James tells us "to him that knoweth to do good, and doeth it not, to him it is sin" (James 4:17, KJV).

A sixth thing that will weaken your faith is not walking with God. This could be not faith-walking daily, or perhaps not being faithful to Sunday gatherings of believers. To walk with God is to be near/close to God. That is why the Scriptures exhort us to "draw near to God, and He will draw near to you" (James 4:8).

Our closeness to God is a reflection of our heart attitude. When our hearts are open/warm to God, then we want to get close to Him. If there is sin in your life, you do one of two things. You either face it and deal with it by confessing and/or repentance, or, if you do nothing about your sin, you will find yourself moving away from God ... from His presence ... from doing His will. Nothing takes the place of walking in close fellowship with God so that you have fellowship with Him on a continuing basis.

The seventh thing that will weaken your faith is being drawn away by satan. The adversary is smart and knows how to blind/detract us from faith-walking with Jesus. He can put other thoughts of sin into our minds so that we forget about God and fellowshipping with Him. Or satan can just keep us so busy we never have time to think about or call out to the Lord. James tells us to "resist the devil and he will flee from you" (James 4:7).

The eighth reason your faith is weak is because you have not used it. As we daily pray in faith, we exercise our faith and it becomes strengthened. But if we don't apply our faith—we let it lie dormant—then our faith becomes useless and begins to die. This involves not acting in faith, not praying in faith.

The ninth thing that weakens your faith is expressed in the statement "you have not because you ask not" (James 4:2). You don't exercise your faith and you don't pray. This means you may have faith but you haven't acted on your faith, or you have not used your faith. To put it another way, even if you have faith, or you have gained a certain strength of faith, you will lose it if you don't use it.

This is a comparison to muscle strength. You must use your muscles regularly/daily to keep the strength you have. To increase your faith or muscle strength, you must add muscle exercise, correct diet, proper rest, and other items included in maintaining good health. So, keep using your faith to keep it at its present strength. To get more faith strength, then doing the items listed above will strengthen muscles and/or faith.

The tenth thing to weaken your faith is "harboring idols." John the apostle warns, "Little children, keep yourself from idols" (1 John 5:21). Usually an idol is worshipped or exalted in one's life. John was referring to an image carved out of stone or wood. But an idol doesn't have to be a thing; it can be anything that takes the place of God. Instead of obeying God, worshipping God, and putting God first in your life, when you place anything in first place—God's place—you have made/created it into an idol.

And what does an idol do? An idol controls your life, including your time, energy, money, resources, everything. When you let anything take God's place, you make it a substitute idol. It becomes an idol that controls your life.

What is wrong with this picture? You should control your life with self-discipline ... self-direction. Then make sure you yield yourself to Christ so that He controls your life. Let Jesus indwell you and His power flow through you to glorify the heavenly Father.

Those who have an idol have something foreign controlling their life. It is not you, the other thing/person is at the center of your life, and it is not Christ who wants to transform you so you will glorify the heavenly Father. An idol is anything that controls your life. Since Christ has given you eternal life, a satisfying life, and His indwelling, then why would you let anything, or any person, or any idol control your life?

The eleventh thing to weaken your faith is an unforgiving spirit. Jesus explained, "... if you have anything against anyone, forgive him, that your Father in heaven may also forgive you" (Mark 11:25). Why will an unforgiving spirit destroy your faith? Remember, your faith is your relationship to God. But an unforgiving spirit can mean anger ... hatred ... plans of retaliation ... or revenge. When that spirit makes you want to destroy someone else, be careful; it could destroy you.

An unforgiving spirit usually does not just sit in our inner personality. It festers. It grows with time so that we grow more angry, and we want to retaliate even greater than when that anger first gripped our thoughts. When anger grows, it controls us. Next we show more anger with time, and then we want to retaliate even greater—if that is possible.

Retaliation can eat you up and make you think or do things you had not planned to do. You should not say or think or do anything that Jesus wouldn't do. Remember, Jesus is your example: "To this you were called, because Christ ... leaving us an example, that you should follow His steps" (1 Peter 2:21).

The twelfth thing that weakens your faith is the principle of selfishness. If you won't/don't help others with their needs, then you will not receive help in your time of need. Proverbs tells us, "Whoever shuts his ears to the cry of the poor, will also cry himself and not be heard"

(Proverbs 21:13). Remember, God sees all things, knows all our needs, and sees all our responses to people in need; therefore, if we don't help the needy when we could/should help them, then God has a basis for not helping us in our time of need. Of course, your repentance at any-time for any sin or omission you have committed will be heard by God.

Let's reverse the old saying "God helps those who help themselves." While there is some truth in that statement, it shows promise: "God helps those who help others."

What is your priority? Your first priority is God: He comes first in all you do and in all things. Second, others: let your focus be on helping others. Third, self: but remember, when you surrender "self" to God so that He is first, then you will enjoy all things that glorify God, for God is your primary focus.

The thirteenth thing to weaken your faith is not honoring family relationships. What is God's formula for a married couple? "Husbands, love your wives, just as Christ also loved the church and gave Himself for her" (Ephesians 5:25). Then, "Wives, submit to your own husbands, as to the Lord" (Ephesians 5:22). This means that when you violate family obligations and create family problems, it weakens the faith of either husband or wife.

The first is, the husband must love his wife as Christ loved the church. What kind of love did Jesus have? Sacrificial love ... giving love ... love that overlooks mistakes and problems ... love that never gives up. If your faith has the same qualities as this love, then you have overcoming faith. But if your faith flounders, it will resemble the love found in some mar-riages, i.e., selfish faith and complaining faith.

Your relationship to each other—husband and wife—should resem-ble your faith to God. And what kind of faith is that? Forgiving faith ... understanding faith ... patient faith ... and sacrificial faith.

The fourteenth thing that will weaken faith is when your faith is directed at the wrong object. Your faith has its source in God and you receive your faith from Him. But also, your faith is directed toward God. The writers of Hebrews noted, "without faith it is impossible to please God" (Hebrews 11:6). After all, faith is a relationship with God, and your relationship to God is bonded by your faith. You cannot please God without faith; that means you cannot come into His presence, have access in prayer, and stand righteous in His presence without faith. That means your faith gives you all three: access to His presence, answers to prayer, standing justified in His presence.

The fifteenth thing that weakens your faith is improper reverence to God. Remember, reverencing God is fearing Him. The psalmist declared, "He will fulfill the desires of them that fear Him, He will hear their cry" (Psalm 145:19).

Why would you fear God? Because He is a holy God who can cast anyone into hell as punishment for their sins(s). But you come to God through Jesus Christ, who died for your sins and was raised from the dead to give you eternal life. In Jesus you are forgiven ... given eternal life ... a home in Heaven ... and the privilege of serving the Father. How can you do that? Because Jesus lives in you and indwells you with His power (see Galatians 2:20).

Now you approach the Father not in weakened faith but with the "faith of the Son of God who loves me and gave Himself for me" (Galatians 2:20). When you have Jesus in your heart, you have His faith, which is stronger than your faith. The faith of Jesus in you will guarantee everything you need to serve God and that you will go to live with Him in Heaven.

The sixteenth thing to weaken your faith is insincere faith. What is that? It is faith that is half-hearted, meaning not focused completely on God. It is also faith without intensity. Paul tells us to "do it heartily, as to the Lord" (Colossians 3:23). Again Paul exhorts us, "laboring fervently

... in prayers" (Colossians 4:12). Here Paul is explaining that insincere faith will not work, nor bring you results.

The seventeenth thing that will weaken your faith is not praying with others or agreeing with others for an answer to prayer. Jesus said, "Again I say to you that if two of you agree on earth concerning anything that they ask, it will be done for them by My Father in heaven" (Matthew 18:19). When two people agree together and ask in prayer together, Jesus said, "It shall be done for them." Why did Jesus make this promise? The next verse declares, "where two or three are gathered together in My name, I am there in the midst of them" (v. 20). What a great promise. Not that our prayer would be heard or answered, but that Jesus's presence would be in our midst as we pray.

Have you obeyed Jesus to pray with another/many believers? Their faith will strengthen you, as you strengthen them. Have you obeyed Jesus by asking or making your prayers to Him? Do you expect an answer(s)? God wants to grow your faith, hear your prayers, and answer them. But is God waiting on you to begin?

The eighteenth thing that will weaken your faith is your lack of abiding in Jesus. He invited us to "abide in Me as I abide in you" (John 15:3). To abide in Jesus is having a face-to-face relationship with Him. Then abiding in Jesus is knowing and obeying the Scriptures (see John 15:7). What does abiding do for you? "That you bear much fruit" (John 15:5). First, your fruit is your character or your testimony (see Galatians 5:22-23). Second, your fruit is when you win someone to Jesus (see 2 Corinthians 5:11).

The nineteenth thing that will weaken your faith is spiritual blindness. Before we were saved, sin blinded our spiritual eyes and we did not understand or apply the Scriptures to our lives. "The god [satan] of this age has blinded, who do not believe" (2 Corinthians 4:4). When the message of Jesus was preached to us, our spiritual eyes were opened by the power of the gospel. Remember, Jesus said, "I am the light of the world" (John 8:12). He helps us see our sin and gives us power to repent and turn to Him. Jesus then helps us see/understand His death that forgave our sins and cleansed our hearts. Finally, Jesus helps us see Himself; He is our salvation.

The great internal miracle is when your blindness is removed and you see Jesus your Savior. He saved you and gives you eternal life. And as you stand in Jesus's presence, remember that He took away your spiritual blindness.

The twentieth thing that will weaken your faith is when you quit praying and you give up too soon. Paul tells us, "continue in prayer" (Colossians 4:2). He also tells us, "Pray without ceasing" (1 Thessalonians 5:17). As you pray in faith, don't give up. As you look to God for answers, keep your faith strong. But if you give up and quit praying, that weakens your faith. Your lack of prayer could be the weak link that keeps answers from coming.

The twenty-first thing is giving into your old nature. Jesus reminded us, "The spirit is willing but the flesh is weak" (Matthew 26:41). When God wants to do something for you, make sure you don't quit too soon. Don't quit praying ... don't quit exercising faith ... don't give up hope.

CONCLUSION

There are many things that will weaken your faith; don't let any of the items mentioned in this chapter hold you back. But just as there are at least 21 things that can weaken your faith, there are just that many that will strengthen your faith.

Remember, you are making a faith statement as you keep doing what is right and don't give in to the things that will weaken your faith. God wants your faith strengthened because He wants to work in you and through you. God also wants His work to go forward, and He needs you and me to strengthen our faith ... not give in ... and keep our eyes on Jesus.

Chapter 7

HOW TO GROW YOUR FAITH

Your faith grows exceedingly.

2 Thessalonians 1:3

WHEN Paul wrote his second letter to the believers in Thessalonica, he was thankful for several things; but he mentioned first of all that their faith was growing, using the adverb "exceedingly." Their faith was growing so rapidly and so large that it could be described as abundant faith.

Paul also thanked God that their love was abounding and that their patience was strong in persecutions and tribulations. Remember, Paul had gone to Thessalonica to plant a church and only stayed there three weeks before rioters drove him out of the city. The spiritual growth of the Thessalonians was much greater than what he expected; it had grown abundantly.

Now your faith can grow because it is a seed that naturally grows when planted. Didn't Jesus remind us, "faith as a grain of mustard seed" (Matthew 17:20)? So, when faith is planted and begins to grow, it is small. Didn't Jesus describe those who have little faith? "O you of little faith" (Matthew 14:31). Paul also described this condition as those who had "weak faith" (Romans 14:1).

When you find some with little or weak faith that grows to strong faith, you will be reminded of the story of Abraham in Scripture: "Abraham ... was strong in faith" (Romans 4:20). Therefore, we conclude that Paul was not exaggerating when he said, "your faith grows exceedingly" (2 Thessalonians 1:3).

We should have known that faith had life, and faith can grow, and faith can reproduce itself. Paul described that reproduction: "from faith to faith" (Romans 1:17).

This description also suggests there are different expressions of faith, so you can begin with weak faith and grow to strong faith. Also, faith can grow from saving faith to walking by faith. Then your faith can be studied because it is called doctrinal faith. But not just rational faith or understanding—you can have indwelling faith that lives in you the believer (see Galatians 2:20). This faith is described as the "faith of Christ" that Jesus gives us when He comes to live in our hearts. Then it becomes our personal faith, because Jesus lives within the saved individual.

10 PRINCIPLES TO GROW YOUR FAITH

The following ten principles are not listed in any one place in Scripture but are found throughout Scripture. These ten principles are seen in the lives of those who lived and served by faith, but they are also found expressed as commands, or instructions, or descriptions of faith growth.

1. Grow Your Faith with Prayer.

The disciples recognized their lack of faith, so they asked Jesus—today's form of prayer—"Lord, increase our faith" (Luke 17:5).

But praying for faith is more than just asking for it. When you ask God to teach you how to serve Him, aren't you asking for greater faith? And when you pray for God to use your ministry, are you not also asking for faith? When you pray for insight to learn or understand God's Word, aren't you asking for more faith to apply the Word of God to your life or ministry? And when you are trying to serve the Lord, don't you ask Him to help you minister, or you ask God to use your efforts? Isn't that another way of praying for faith?

As you study the Bible, you want to fulfill Paul's exhortation to "study to show yourself approved unto God, a workman that doesn't need to be ashamed" (2 Timothy 2:15). As you apply your mind to know Scripture, aren't you at the same time asking God to help you understand His Word?

We all need discipline to live and walk for the Lord. When you begin applying self-control to various parts of your life, you naturally think/talk to yourself about what you want to do. Isn't that conversation an expression of faith that you want God's help in self-discipline?

As you pray for experience to search abilities to serve the Lord, isn't that another way of expressing the faith prayer?

Finally, we all seek courage or wisdom to face the challenges of life and ministry. Isn't our seeking these inner strengths an expression of faith? Aren't we asking God to give us courage or wisdom?

2. Grow Your Faith by Planting God's Word in Your Heart.

You cannot separate the two, i.e., the Bible and faith. "Faith comes by hearing... the Word of God" (Romans 10:17). Years ago someone taught me five ways to use the Bible to grow my faith. The person counted these five ways on the fingers of his hand, beginning at the littlest finger, the one we call the *pinky*. Obviously, the strongest finger is the thumb, and on the below list are ways to grow your faith. The last—meditate—gives us the accumulated strength of all the fingers.

1. <u>**Pinky—Hear the Bible**</u>. Usually, we first learn new lessons by hearing. Why? Because our ears hear everything about us, even the things we cannot see with our eyes. John wrote, "Blessed is he who ... hears the words of this prophecy" (Revelation 1:3). Hearing is probably the first effective way to communicate with a physical baby, and with a newborn in Christ.

2. <u>**Ring man—Read**</u>. The same verse used previously included the exhortation to read the words of Scripture: "Blessed is he who reads the words of this prophecy" (Revelation 1:3). Reading takes more energy than hearing the Word of God, and reading takes training to master its skills. Once you master the art of reading, you can associate words with meaning, and the words of Scripture begin to take on spiritual meaning/understanding.

3. <u>**Tall man—Study**</u>. Studying is the third step to understand the Scriptures, and you will develop faith from the Word of God. Paul tells us plainly, "Study to shew thyself approved unto God, a workman that needeth not to be ashamed, rightly dividing the word of truth" (2 Timothy 2:15, KJV). What does studying the Scriptures involve? Time to read the passage several times. Analyzing the passage word by word, then finding the meaning of each word. But most of all, study involves putting together everything you have learned into a sentence/thought so you can remember what you studied.

4. <u>**Pointer—Memorize**</u>. The fourth step in studying Scripture is to commit to memory what you have learned. The book of Psalms tells how a young Christian can become rooted/grow in their faith. "How can a young man cleanse his way? By taking heed according to Your word ... Your word I have hidden in my heart,

that I might not sin against You" (Psalm 119:9,11). So memory is more than the ability to repeat the word/symbols of a verse. You memorize a verse so its meaning becomes a part of your heart/life.

5. **Thumb—Meditate**. Because you have memorized and studied the Bible, it is in your mind/heart. Now you will apply the Bible to your daily life as you meditate on the words of Scripture. Paul tells young Timothy, "Meditate on these things" (1 Timothy 4:15). The first psalm describes the believer who is like a living tree that brings forth fruit. That believer's "delight is in the law of the Lord, and in that law he meditates day and night" (Psalm 1:3).

3. Grow Your Faith by Obeying God.

To understand how your faith gets stronger, look at the muscles of the human body. They get healthier and stronger with proper exercise. So how does the human body get stronger? By obedience/application. As you regularly stretch your faith, it will grow. But you must exercise according to the direction of the Word of God.

Look at what builds up our physical muscles and apply these principles to your faith. First, by daily or continuous exercise. You won't grow your faith to be strong by just going to church one day a week. You need daily exercise by following God.

Next, repetitive exercise. Just as you do the same thing in the gym to grow physical muscles, so too stretch your faith daily by repetitive exercise. Trust God for new things. Pray for greater answers to prayer. Stretch your faith to learn more Scriptures.

Did I just say stretch? Yes, stretching is reaching for a new answer to prayer, or a new insight from the Bible, or a new level of ministry. All new accomplishments lead to growth of the muscles or the growth of faith.

4. Grow Your Faith by Looking to Jesus.

As we walk in faith, we are exhorted to look "unto Jesus the author and finisher of our faith" (Hebrews 12:1). This book has talked about faith-walking. How do you do it? By walking and looking at the same time.

Are you just beginning to faith-walk? Think of a little baby who is about to take his/her first step. First, the baby lets go of the parent/one holding him/her. Then the baby stands by him/herself for a moment. Second, the baby looks at the one who is waiting for him/her. They might be holding out waiting arms. The baby sees the arms waiting for him/her or sees the distance, which is the third thing. Then a step is taken. The baby is no longer supported by the adult who first stands him/her up. The baby has not yet grabbed hold of the next person waiting for him/her. The baby takes his/her first step and walks. Maybe not strong steps or steady steps, but nevertheless he/she walks.

If you are going to walk by faith, your focus should not be on your problems or obstacles. Yes, you will have to deal with them, but your focus should be on where you are going and your determination to get there. When Peter was in the boat during the storm, he saw Jesus walking on the water. Peter cried out, "Lord, bid me come to You." Jesus gave him a command: "Come." Peter stepped out of the boat and walked on the water. "But when he [Peter] saw the wind was boisterous" (Matthew 14:30), it was then he began to sink. He took his eyes off Jesus and focused on the problem, i.e., winds and waves. So faith-walking involves going to Jesus with your eyes on Him.

5. Grow Your Faith by Yielding to the Indwelling Christ.

We who are believers have an inner strength, which is the indwelling Christ. "I have been crucified with Christ; it is no longer I who live, but Christ lives in me; and the life which I now live in the flesh I live by faith

---

in the Son of God, who loved me and gave Himself for me" (Galatians 2:20). Once Christ indwells you, He has the strength to give you victory. "I can do all things through Christ who strengthens me" (Philippians 4:13).

6. Grow Your Faith by Constantly Seeking the Lord.

Why will seeking the Lord build your faith? Because seeking God is answering/obeying the Lord. "When You said, 'Seek My face,' my heart said to You, 'Your face, Lord, I will seek'" (Psalm 27:8). How do you seek? The same way you look for something you have lost in your house. You don't start looking everywhere down the street or in another town. No! You look where you lost it, or where it might be located. But you look continuously until you find it. Seeking God is a continuous attitude of your heart and mind. You seek God until you find Him.

Jesus tells us that seeking will result in answers to prayer. He told us, "Ask, and it will be given to you; seek, and you will find; knock, and it will be opened to you" (Matthew 7:7). So, with your seeking, add asking and knocking, which are expressions of prayer. Remember, prayer is talking with God because we have a relationship with Him. Just tell God what you want/need.

7. Grow Your Faith by Constant Claiming of the Blood of Christ.

The Bible promises that when you faith-walk in the light of Jesus Christ, you will have the constant cleansing of Jesus's blood. "But if we walk in the light as He is in the light, we have fellowship with one another, and the blood of Jesus Christ His Son cleanses us from all sin" (1 John 1:7). So, from this passage, faith-walking and light-walking are the same. That is because you are following Jesus your Savior. Your faith eyes are on Him.

Notice the three conditions for faith-walking. All three begin with the word "if." First, "if we walk in the light" (1:7)—that means you are following Jesus and the Word of God. Second, "If we say we have not sinned' (1:8)—that means you must recognize your past sin; when you recognize your sin problem, you begin to solve your biggest problem.

The third "if" is when we recognize and confess our sins and deal with them in God's presence. "If we confess our sins, He is faithful and just to forgive us *our* sins and to cleanse us from all unrighteousness" (1 John 1:9). So God will forgive us and accept us into His fellowship.

WHAT TO DO WITH YOUR SIN

Confess it to God.

Repent and not do it again.

Learn from it.

8. Grow Your Faith by Trusting God, Not Yourself.

Remember, we are challenged to faith-walk because "faith without works is dead" (James 2:20). So your walking is the second half of this verse. We could interpret this verse "faith works." You begin with faith before you start to serve God.

9. Grow Your Faith by Surrendering to God.

When you yield yourself to God, you surrender and let the power of Christ flow through you (see Galatians 2:20). Paul explains that this act of yielding ourselves to God is when "You give yourselves completely to God ... use your body as an instrument to do what is right" (Romans 6:13-14, NLT). It is then the power of Christ flows through you with two forces: first, the power to do what is right, and second, the power to not do what is sin/wrong.

10. Grow Your Faith by Showing Gratitude.

It was once said, "Gratitude is the least remembered of all virtues." Yes, the virtue of gratitude is usually the last we develop, but it is the foundation for all other virtues. Paul told the Colossians, "So walk in Him ... established in the faith ... with thanksgiving" (Colossians 2:6-7). So, when your positive attitude controls your life, you can be victorious over problems and adversity.

So how does gratitude work? It changes your inner energy into a positive approach to life. Just as letting Christ live in the center of your life helps you overcome any barrier to live for Him, so too when Christ controls your life, you will find gratitude is present to control the rest of your life.

PART TWO

FAITH
WALKING
with
JESUS

DEVOTIONS

Day 1

FAITH TO SPEAK

So Jesus answered and said to them, "Have faith in God. For assuredly, I say to you, whoever says to this mountain, 'Be removed and be cast into the sea,' and does not doubt in his heart, but believes that those things he says will be done, he will have whatever he says."

Mark 11:22-23

JESUS challenged His disciples to move a mountain by *saying* to the mountain *move*. Now you don't have within you the power to move a physical mountain. No! So what did Jesus mean? The power to move a mountain—physical problems or obstacles blocking your ministry—this is what Jesus meant. So where does the power come from? God! The next question is, how do you get God to move a mountain for you? The answer is, believe that these things happen. Let's reduce the explanation to one word: "faith." Do you have faith to move the mountain blocking your ministry or the things you want to do in life? If you said no, then this lesson/series is for you. You get *mountain-moving power* from God.

Lord, I confess I don't have strong faith. Sometimes I feel my faith is so weak, I cannot find it. I pray with the man in Scripture, "Lord, increase my faith." Amen.

When Jesus described mountain-moving faith, He was referring to the obstacles/problems we face in our ministry/life. Since Jesus has saved you from your sins, that is the greatest power of all—because it involved breaking the chains of hell. Thank God for breaking these chains! Now thank God for His mountain-moving power. If you meant it when you thanked God for it, then ask Him to use it in your life.

Lord, I know You have forgiven my sins and broken the power of satan in my life. Now I ask for Your power to remove barriers and obstacles that keep me from serving You fully. Amen.

READ:

Hebrews 11:1-40

Day 2

MOUNTAIN-MOVING FAITH

So Jesus answered and said to them, "Have faith in God. For assuredly, I say to you, whoever says to this mountain, 'Be removed and be cast into the sea,' and does not doubt in his heart, but believes that those things he says will be done, he will have whatever he says."

Mark 11:22-23

JESUS challenged His disciples to move mountains by faith. He was not talking about a physical mountain like Mount Everest, but the mountains—barriers—in Christian ministry or in your personal life. A mountain barrier could be physical or political problems stopping the work of God, like man-made laws, opposition from individuals motivated by evil, social movements, or space limitations. Sometimes barriers are internal, and our faith must first overcome our inward resistance to what God wants to do; or barriers could come completely from the outside. The solution is our faith attacking our mountain problems—"be moved."

Lord, I have both big and small problems in my life. Help me grow my faith bigger than my barriers. Then help me serve You and praise You for victory. Help me follow Your leading in my life. Amen.

We will always have problems—big and small—facing us in our personal life, as well as in serving the Lord. We need *faith mentality* to believe God has an answer for us. Then we need *faith application* to apply God's solution to our barriers. Finally, we must end up with *faith gratitude* when we thank God for His help and praise Him for answers. Finally we need *worship faith* to come into His presence to adore Him.

Lord, I pray with the disciples, "increase our faith" (Luke 17:5). Teach me to look at problems with faith eyes and help me as I apply faith answers to the problems and barriers of life. Amen.

READ:

Mark 11:12-26

Day 3

WHAT IS MORE
THAN FAITH?

*If I had the gift of prophecy, and if I understood
all of God's secret plans and possessed all
knowledge, and if I had such faith that I could
move mountains, but didn't love others, I would
be nothing. Three things will last forever—faith,
hope, and love—and the greatest of these is love.*

1 Corinthians 13:2,13, NLT

IF you had faith to move mountains but didn't love, what would you
be? If you could raise millions of dollars by faith but didn't love, what
would you be? If you could pray or preach by faith for millions to be
saved but didn't love, what would you be? If you could build the largest,
most powerful church in the world but didn't love, what would you be?
Could you do anything worthwhile for God if you didn't love? Impossible questions to answer in our human body. But remember, when you
ask God for faith—or you ask in faith—remember love. Why? Paul
said, "I would gain nothing without love" (v. 3, ELT).

> *Lord, as I pray for great faith, I also ask for great love. Help
> me to exercise faith as Your heroes in the Bible. But more im-
> portantly, help me love as Jesus loves. He loved the Father;*

He loves the world (see John 3:16); He loves me and gave Himself for me. Amen.

Don't measure your faith by what you do or by what you accomplish: measure your faith by the object of your faith—God. Your faith is no greater that the God who answers your faith. So, to move God with your faith, become like God in your heart and with your desires—love. Remember, "God is love" (1 John 4:7). When you love like God, He will use your faith to move mountains.

Lord, forgive my selfish faith and selfish love that is centered on me. Forgive me ... cleanse me by the blood of Christ ... accept me ... guide me ... use me. Give me Your love so I can love others. Amen.

READ:

1 Corinthians 13:1-13

Day 4

THE SIZE OF
YOUR FAITH

*The apostles said to the Lord, "Show us how to
increase our faith." The Lord answered, "If you had
faith even as small as a mustard seed, you could say
to this mulberry tree, 'May you be uprooted and
be planted in the sea,' and it would obey you!"*

Luke 17:5-6, NLT

IF you ask God for faith, how much do you need? Sometimes we think we need more faith—in gigantic proportions—to serve God. But Jesus knows that either you have faith in God or you do not. The answer is not getting more faith; the solution is using the faith in God you already have. The answer to your prayers and the solutions to your needs are God Himself. Either you know God or you don't. Either you believe in God or you don't. If you have faith so small as a mustard seed—so tiny you can barely see it—you can move a huge sycamore tree or a mountain (see Mark 11:22-23). Why? Because it is God who does the work, not you. All you do is believe.

*Lord, I believe in You and my head tells me You are power-
ful and almighty. But at times I doubt. I pray with the man*

in Scripture, "I believe, help Thou mine unbelief" (Mark 9:24, KJV). Amen.

So we don't pray for more faith; we need to pray for spiritual eyes to see God ... see His power ... see His potential ... see our relationship to Him. So it is not our faith that moves the mountains; it is a powerful God who moves the sycamore tree or mountains. Either you have faith in God or you don't. How lame/small is your faith?

Lord, my faith is small, and sometimes I cannot see it or feel it—but I feel You. Help me get my eyes off myself and give me faith—eyes to see You and trust You. Amen.

READ:

Luke 17:1-37

Day 5

FAITH TO MOVE OBSTACLES

Thought I have all faith ... to move mountain.

1 Corinthians 13:2

*So, Jesus said ..., "if you have faith as a
mustard seed, you will say to this mountain,
'Move from here to there,' and it will move;
and nothing will be impossible for you."*

Matthew 17:20

ONE of the benefits of faith is that it can remove obstacles that stop the work of God or hinder the growth of spirituality in God's followers. Notice the conditional word "if": *if* you have faith as small as a mustard seed. Quickly remember, a mustard seed is so small you can lose it under your fingernail. With that small amount of faith, Jesus promises you can move mountains/barriers. Faith so small it can be lost under your fingernail can remove the biggest obstacles in your life that are holding back your ministry, or your effectiveness, or your spiritual growth. What is under your fingernail? How big is your faith?

Lord, my problems in life seem bigger than a mountain, and my faith is small. Give me faith when I don't have any. Strengthen my faith because it is small. Teach me to use my faith to remove the obstacles that are keeping me from serving and growing. Amen.

Often the Bible observes our small faith as "little faith" (Matthew 14:31), and "small as a mustard seed" (Matthew 17:20), and "weak faith" (Romans 14:1). Even though tiny, your small faith is powerful—not because of your ability, but because of God. God can do anything He wants to do. So your tiny faith can motivate a powerful God to do what He wants done.

Lord, I confess my faith is small. I know You are big and powerful. I look to You to remove the obstacles blocking my spiritual growth or hindering my ministry. I call upon Your power to accomplish Your work. And may You receive all the glory for the answers/solutions You send. Amen.

READ:

1 Corinthians 13:1-13

Day 6

WHAT FAITH?

*For I am not ashamed of the gospel of Christ, for it
is the power of God to salvation for everyone who
believes, for the Jew first and also for the Greek. For
in it the righteousness of God is revealed from faith
to faith; as it is written, "The just shall live by faith."*

Romans 1:16-17

DID you see the statement "from faith to faith" (Romans 1:17)?
It tells you to grow/go from one expression of faith to another.
But which one? Most will say saving faith is the beginning and
we go/grow into daily faith, which is "walking by faith" (2 Corinthians
5:7). But the theologian will tell us to begin with *doctrinal faith,* which
includes the content we must believe to go to Heaven. Then we move to
justifying faith, which declares us perfect or righteous before God. Still
other practical believers will tell us we begin following Jesus with *daily
faith* and then serve Him by using our spiritual gift of faith, which is
serving faith. Does the author of Romans mean a specific order of faith?
Or did he suggest we interpret the kind of faith mentioned in this verse
according to our need? What do you think?

*Lord, faith is simply learning about You, accepting You, and
following You. My faith resulted in a new and meaning-*

ful relationship with you. To me it is all relationship faith. Amen.

We learn faith from the way it is spelled: F-A-I-T-H. This acrostic means "**F**orsaking **A**ll, **I T**ake **H**im." Yes, that is faith. I let go of everything else and I cling only to Jesus. Technically, it is *Jesus faith*. Is there any other faith that will help/transform your life on Earth? Is there any other faith that will take you to live with God in Heaven when you die? No! Faith is simply *relating to Jesus*.

Lord Jesus, I thank You for saving me. Now I will follow You every day. I thank You for justifying faith that gives me perfect standing in Your sight. I will walk by faith ... live by faith ... minister by faith ... and I will go to Heaven with this faith. Amen.

READ:

Romans 1:1-17

Day 7

KEEPING THE FAITH

*I have fought the good fight, I have finished
the race, I have kept the faith.*

2 Timothy 4:7

PAUL uses the article "the" when referring to objective faith, which is doctrinal faith, i.e., the object of his faith. This is referring to the content of what Paul believed. Paul was first converted on the road to Damascus by *saving faith.* Up until then Paul not only believed all the Old Testament content, but he also defended it and persecuted any who added faith in Jesus Christ. But when Paul was saved, not only did he add to his life *saving faith* but also Christ came to live in Paul. He added *indwelling faith.* Now in today's verse Paul is explaining his allegiance to both Old and New Testament faith. Paul not only believed all he knew about Christ, but he now also defended it; and in today's phrases, Paul says he "kept the faith."

*Lord, may I be as faithful as Paul. I believe all that the Old
and New Testaments teach about Jesus Christ. I will live it
... defend it ... teach it; and as Paul said, I will keep it. It is
because I have Jesus in my heart, who saved me. Amen.*

The word "kept" means more than keep it wrapped up in your memory or heart; it means you have learned the faith ... and you live the faith

... and you tell others about the faith. Now part of "the faith" is the Great Commission to go ... tell ... all the world. So, to "keep the faith" means sharing the message of faith with lost people.

Lord, I will keep the faith in my heart, then I will keep the faith in my daily life. Next I will keep the faith in my ministry. And finally, I will keep the faith by looking for Christ's return for me. Amen.

READ:

2 Timothy 4:1-18

Day 8

FROM FAITH
TO FAITH

*For I am not ashamed of the gospel of Christ, for it
is the power of God to salvation for everyone who
believes, for the Jew first and also for the Greek. For
in it the righteousness of God is revealed from faith
to faith; as it is written, "The just shall live by faith."*

Romans 1:16-17

D ID you see that Paul boasted of his faith in Jesus Christ? He was
not ashamed of God's power that transformed him. It comes by
faith. When Paul described "from faith to faith," he was explaining the various ways our faith reaches God to unleash His transforming
mercy into our lives. First, faith is objective. It is the content of the Bible
that must be believed to be saved. Second, when we exercise saving faith,
we are born again into God's family. The third type of faith recognizes
the completed accomplishment of Jesus on the cross that forgave our
sins and declared we were justified, or made perfect in the Father's sight
(see Romans 5:1).

*Lord, thank You for giving me the Scriptures, through which
I gain faith. And thank You for Christ's death to provide
saving faith so that I am delivered from hell. Beyond that,*

*thank You for justifying faith that gives me the righteousness
to stand in Your presence. Amen.*

Next, God placed *indwelling faith* in your heart for godly living. That faith is none other than the faith of Jesus in our heart, which gives us power to serve Him. Then I can live daily by faith, claiming all the benefits listed above. Finally, I am given the spiritual gift of faith to live and serve Jesus Christ.

*Lord, thank You for giving me simple faith to believe in You.
This faith has many expressions. Help me to learn all about
each one and give me Your grace to apply each faith to my life.
May I please You by living and claiming all faith. Amen.*

READ:

Romans 1:1-17

Day 9

YOUR THREE INNER POWERS

Thank God! Once you were slaves of sin, but now you wholeheartedly obey this teaching we have given you.

Romans 6:17, NLT

WHAT is involved in *saving faith?* Or to express it another way, how must you respond to God to be converted to go to Heaven? You must respond with all that is within you. God doesn't want a half-hearted response, and He doesn't only want part of your life. He wants all of you. First, you have the power of an intellectual mind that receives, recognizes, interprets, and understands data. That is the ability to know. God wrote the message of Jesus and His plan of salvation in the Bible so you can understand salvation. Next, God created us with an emotional power to feel, experience, and yes, to both love and hate. Our salvation involves loving God ... enjoying Him ... and embracing Him with our feelings.

Lord, I use my mind to learn about You, always yielding my intellect so You will come fill my mind with Yourself. And, Lord, I also yield my emotions to You. Come live in my feelings ... my love ... my joy ... and my fear of displeasing You. Amen.

The third power in your world is your ability to make decisions. You can desire godliness and reject evil. Our powerful will is driven by what we know in our minds and what we feel in our emotions. These three powers—intellect, emotion, and will—control your destiny: where you live, what you do, and what you make of your life. But these three also control the mistakes you make and the problems you create.

Lord, I yield my inner person to You—intellect, emotions, and will. Come live in the center of my life. Guard me from mistakes, but most importantly guide me to do all things to glorify You. Amen.

READ:

Romans 6:1-23

Day 10

TRUE FAITH

*Now the Holy Spirit tells us clearly that in
the last times some will turn away from the
true faith; they will follow deceptive spirits
and teachings that come from demons.*

1 Timothy 4:1, NLT

WHEN the article "the" is used with faith in this verse, it is
called "the true faith." The "true faith" is the content of the
Word of God. You must believe it. Why is it true? Because
its core is Jesus, who said, "I am the ... truth" (John 14:6). If you want
the true way to Heaven, it is Jesus. Why? Because He died for your sins
and was raised on the third day to give you new life—His eternal life.
Paul said that some had departed from *the true faith*, which carries a
warning to you: be faithful to the content of the true faith; be faithful
till death.

> *Lord, I believe what is written in the Bible. That is the mes-
> sage that has transformed my life. I know I was lost and I
> know I lived in sin; but when I believed in Jesus and accept-
> ed Him as my Savior, I was given a new nature, and now I
> have Jesus living in my heart. Amen.*

Paul described those who "departed from the faith," meaning they gave up their allegiance to Jesus and His written Word of God. To leave one is to leave both, and Paul had concerns for those who "left the faith." Why was he concerned? Their eternal souls were hanging in the balance. Make sure you hold on to the true faith found in Scripture, and make sure Jesus Christ is living in your heart.

Lord, I learned about the living Word of God—Jesus Christ (see John 1:1-12)—when I accepted the living Jesus Christ into my heart. I have both in my heart and will hold on to both. Amen.

READ:

1 Timothy 4:1-16

Day 11

SEEKERS

*Trust in the Lord with all your heart; do not depend
on your own understanding. Seek His will in all
you do, and He will show you which path to take.*

Proverbs 3:5-6, NLT

BOTH of today's verses have great promises to those who seek God.
Do you seek God ... seek to know Him ... obey Him ... please
Him? This Proverb's verses tell you to trust in the Lord first and
not depend on yourself. Have you trusted Him today? The second part
of that verse says that God will show you what path to take when you
seek Him. Does that mean a total life path? Yes, but you must seek Him
continually. Does that mean God will guide you today, i.e., a daily plan
of living? Yes, but have you sought Him? Does that mean the very next
step? Yes, you must seek Him day by day and step by step. Need we say,
breath by breath?

*Lord, I will seek You year by year. Give me my life's plan. But
also I will seek You day by day. As I follow, I will seek You
today. I won't rule out breath by breath. Yes, Lord, just as I
trusted You a few seconds ago, now I am trusting You again.
Amen.*

God promises, "seek ... He will show you which path to follow" (v. 6). So, when you missed God's plan, did you seek Him? Pledge now to seek God for your whole life's plan, for your day-by-day plan, and for your moment-by-moment plan. When you do that, "He will show you ..." (v. 6).

Lord, I confess I have been splotchy in seeking You. Some days I seek You more than others. For some projects I seek You more than others. For spiritual things I seek You more than for secular things. Forgive me for my splotchy faith. Give me great faith. Give me moment-by-moment faith. Amen.

READ:

Proverbs 3:1-35

Day 12

PLEASING GOD

*But without faith it is impossible to please
Him, for he who comes to God must believe
that He is, and that He is a rewarder
of those who diligently seek Him.*

Hebrews 11:6

D O you please God? Or to ask another way, how can you please
God? Paul tells us, "If you confess your faith in Jesus with your
mouth and you believe in your heart, He was raised from the
dead to give you eternal life; you will be saved. For your faith pleases
God, and your confession gives you eternal life" (Romans 10:9-10,
ELT). Therefore, when you begin following Christ, you begin pleasing
God. Then every time you obey in faith, you please God. Also, pray-
ing in faith pleases God. Why? Because our eternal God and Father is
pleased with His Son, Jesus Christ. When you come to Him through
His Son, you please God.

> *Father, thank You for sending Jesus to die for my sins. I have
> believed in Jesus and I am saved. Now I come to You through
> Your Son, Jesus Christ. Accept me as You accept Your Son. I
> come praying to You through the intercession of Jesus. Amen.*

When you come to the Father through Jesus Christ, you have all the privileges Heaven can bestow. So worship in faith to magnify both the Father and Jesus. Then live by faith to please both. Then daily pray in faith for all your ministry and needs. Claim the access that Jesus gives you to the Father, and walk daily by faith because you have the power of Jesus living in you (see Galatians 2:20).

> *Father, thank You for all You have done for me through Jesus. I will worship You in faith; then I will pray in faith. Next, I will walk in faith and live daily by faith. I praise both You, the Father, and Jesus, Your Son. Amen.*

READ:

Galatians 2:20–3:13

Day 13

UNBELIEF AND DOUBTS

*The father instantly cried out, "I do believe,
but help me overcome my unbelief!"*

Mark 9:24, NLT

*And it is impossible to please God without
faith. Anyone who wants to come to Him
must believe that God exists and that He
rewards those who sincerely seek Him.*

Hebrews 11:6, NLT

THE two verses above reveal the dilemma facing many believers today. First, they believe in God and come to Him in faith by prayer. But at the same time, they have doubts. They are like the father who told Jesus about the dangers facing his son. Then the father asked, "Help us if you can!" (Mark 9:22). Jesus immediately replied, "What do you mean, 'if I can?'" (v. 23). It is then the father honestly confessed, "I do believe ... help ... my unbelief" (v. 24). Many of us honestly believe in the Lord, but our old sin nature raises a question. If it's not our sin nature, it could be our lack of Bible knowledge to fully trust the heavenly Father.

Lord, I am like the man in Scripture: "I believe ... help my unbelief." Give me more faith; give me more wisdom; give me courage to believe You are the miracle worker. Amen.

When you find your unbelief "popping up" in your faith prayers, immediately confess your unbelief and pray with the disciples, "Lord, increase our faith" (Luke 17:5). That is a valid prayer, but God uses more things to answer that prayer: Scriptures, intercession, obedience, the prayer of faith. Remember, we must grow in Christ, and that involves growing all our abilities to please God: faith, love, ministry, worship.

Lord, I come confessing my unbelief; cleanse me and fill me with Your presence. Give me more faith. Make me strong in my prayer life and lead me in ministry. Be glorified in all I think ... and pray ... and do. Amen.

READ:

Mark 9:1-29

Day 14

FROM FAITH
TO FAITH

For in it the righteousness of God is
revealed from faith to faith; as it is
written, "The just shall live by faith."

Romans 1:17

WHEN Paul wrote the phrase "from faith to faith," did he mean first faith to last faith, or did he mean different expressions of faith? What was Paul trying to tell us? As you study the biblical teachings of Paul, there are six expressions of faith possible for your life, at least six different degrees of strength in faith. The first is *objective faith*, i.e., biblical writings called the principles, "the faith." Jude tells us to defend the Bible: "contend for the faith" (Jude 3, KJV). Next Paul describes *saving faith*: "For by grace are you saved by faith" (Ephesians 2:8). The third is Paul's description of the non-experiential result of faith, i.e., something we don't do for ourselves: when we are "justified by faith" (Romans 5:11) at our conversion. Quickly, add the fourth, indwelling faith, because Christ came in your life at conversion (see Galatians 2:20).

Lord, I love Your salvation that came when I believed in Jesus. Then I enjoyed all the different ways I could express my faith in Jesus Christ. Amen.

The fifth is the challenge to daily live by faith by keeping your eyes on Jesus. You have the power to do that because Jesus lives in your heart and you "can do all things through Christ who strengthens [you]" (Philippians 1:21). The sixth and final expression of faith is called *the gift of faith*. God gives you the spiritual ability to use your talents to serve God.

Lord Jesus, thank You for every expression of faith You have given me. I will faith-walk by keeping my eyes on You and trusting You for daily victory. Amen.

READ:

Romans 12:3-16

Day 15

A BLIND LEAP
OF FAITH

By faith Noah ... prepared an ark.

Hebrews 11:7

For assuredly, I say to you, whoever says to
this mountain, "Be removed and be cast into
the sea," and does not doubt in his heart,
but believes that those things he says will
be done, he will have whatever he says.

Mark 11:23

A leap is described as "to spring free ... from ground ... over an obstacle, to pass from one state to another." Isn't that what Noah did? God warned him the world would be judged by a flood—an event that had never previously happened. His leap of faith was not instantaneous; it took over 100 years to build an ark (a boat to save him, his family, and certain representatives of non-human life). Don't think of Noah's leap, or how long it took to build the ark, or his actions. No! Look for his faith in God, who warned of a coming flood. Noah obeyed the command of God ... immediately ... continually ...

---

completely. Isn't that faith? God has spoken in His Word; by faith obey ... immediately ... continually ... completely.

Lord, thank You for saving the world through Noah, and thank You for his example of faith. Give me the faith of Noah. I need Your help to obey You immediately ... continually ... completely. Help me overcome unbelief. Amen.

The greatness of Noah's faith was his blind obedience to God. No record of rain ... no record of God's judgment on the world ... no church or spiritual community to support his leap of faith that lasted about 100 years. If Noah could do it, why not you?

Lord, I come with strong faith—saving faith. I know You saved me from my sin. Thank You for Jesus's death, which cleansed me from sin. Now I come asking for living faith. Strengthen my daily faith to trust You for daily victories. I believe; "help thou my unbelief" (Mark 9:24, KJV). Amen.

READ:

Genesis 6:1-22

Day 16

HIS LEAP TOOK 50 YEARS

By faith Abraham obeyed when he was
called to go out to the place which he would
receive as an inheritance. And he went
out, not knowing where he was going.

Hebrews 11:8

THINK of Abraham's leap of faith. He was about 50 years old and living in the culture of the fertile crescent of the Euphrates River valley. God told him to leave his homeland ... relatives ... business ... and way of life. God led Abraham to live in the mountains of the holy land, i.e., Palestine. He obeyed traveling about 1,000 miles and settled down among a people he did not know; and later he fought battles to protect his life, family, and property. Why did he do it? Because God called him and led him. Isn't faith obeying God's call and following God's leadership? Isn't faith-walking in close fellowship with God? Abraham's leap of faith was a 50-year journey. Could you take that step of faith? Would you obey in faith?

Lord, thank You for the example of Abraham's faith. Help
me learn from Abraham; help me walk in obedient faith like
Abraham. Abraham had strong faith, and mine is weak.

I want a stronger relationship with You; give me stronger faith. Amen.

Abraham's faith influenced where he lived, how he lived, what he did, and how he related to others. Abraham's faith was at the core of his being and guided all he was and did. Without faith Abraham could not and would not have become the father of the Hebrew people. And remember, Jesus Christ was born in the family line of Abraham.

Lord, Abraham did not know his obedient faith would guide him for 70 years. Give me obedient faith to guide me for the rest of my life. May I walk in relationship faith as did Abraham. Amen.

READ:

Genesis 11:27; 13:4

Day 17

BECAUSE OF HIS FATHER'S FAITH

It was by faith that Isaac promised blessings
for the future to his sons, Jacob and Esau.

Hebrews 11:20, NLT

ISAAC is generally not remembered for his great spiritual victories for God. Most people remember his father, Abraham, and the faith of Abel that led to Isaac's birth when Abraham was 100 years old. Also, people remember Isaac's son Jacob, who fathered 12 sons; and the Hebrew people are remembered as the sons of Jacob. The book of Hebrews only records one act of faith by Isaac: he blessed his sons. That is because, in spite of Isaac's failure, he heard God direct him in a dream. Again, in another night, God came to meet with Isaac (see Genesis 28:12-22) and directed him.

> *Lord, my faith sometimes is weak as the faith of Isaac was*
> *weak at times. Forgive me, cleanse me by the blood of Jesus,*
> *and strengthen my faith. May I rise to serve You and make*
> *a difference in my walk for You, and may I influence others.*
> *Amen.*

When you read the entire life of Isaac, he did not accomplish many great things, and most do not remember much about his life. He had a famous father and famous children. But of course, Isaac's influence is tied to his faithful obedience to his father, Abraham, and to his faith direction to his sons. Can you do the same as Isaac?

Lord, I may not be famous in this life, but I want to live for You ... serve You ... and worship You. I don't know what my children will do for You; all I can do is teach them Your Word and live a godly life before them. Help me learn from Isaac and be faithful to You. Amen.

READ:

Genesis 25:1-24

Day 18

A LEAP/STEP FROM RICHES TO ROYALTY

It was by faith that Moses, when he grew up,
refused to be called the son of Pharaoh's daughter.
He chose to share the oppression of God's people
instead of enjoying the fleeting pleasures of sin.

Hebrews 11:24-25, NLT

NOT all leaps of faith end up in comfortable or pleasant surroundings. Moses took a step toward God and righteous living when he gave up the luxury of Pharaoh's home. He ended up living in the barren wilderness of the Sinai desert. Ultimately, he spent 40 years leading God's people through the desert wilderness. So not everyone who takes a leap of faith ends up in a bed of roses. But Moses gained the inner assurance that he was serving God. He saw daily how he was being used in the work and ministry of God. Beyond that, Moses experienced God's presence and he talked to God face to face (see Exodus 33:12–34:30).

Lord, remind me that my leap of faith is about You and getting closer to You. Remind me that Your presence is greater than any pleasure I could ever enjoy on Earth. I will take a leap of faith to know You and experience Your presence. Amen.

Moses's first leap of faith was walking away from the riches of Egypt to live in the desert for 40 years. Then at age 80 he began the next 40 years serving God as he led God's people to the Promised Land. Moses's leap/step of faith was all about choosing God and putting God's plan first in his life. Would you take the same leap/step?

Lord, thank You for leading me in my life. I have taken several steps/leaps of faith and I have enjoyed Your rewards. I will do it again. Amen.

READ:

Exodus 33:12–34:30

Day 19

A FAITH LEAP INTO
GOD'S HERITAGE

*It was by faith that Rahab the prostitute
was not destroyed with the people in her
city who refused to obey God. For she had
given a friendly welcome to the spies.*

Hebrews 11:31, NLT

RAHAB was a prostitute who sold her body for sexual satisfaction to get money to live. Yet in one encounter with God's servants— spies in Jericho—she put her lot in with God's people. It was a leap/step of faith that paid eternal benefits. First, her faith identified her with the Lord God and His people. Second, it secured safety for her and her family. Third, it carved a plan in Hebrew history. But most importantly, her faith put her in the genealogical line of the Messiah, i.e., Jesus Christ (see Matthew 1:5). All of these benefits were because of one decision for God. Would you have made that decision? Will you in the future?

Lord, thank You for the bravery of Rahab. Give me courage like her to stand against threats to my life. Thank You for her courage. Give me courage like Rahab to choose Your side always and to follow You continually. Amen.

Rahab's faith apparently was gained quickly and her faith was strong enough to hide the spies. Her leap/step of faith was a courageous, death-defying choice. Rahab chose to identify with the Lord God and not with her people. Her faith—instantly displayed—is a testimony to us all. How does Rahab's faith challenge you?

Lord, give me the boldness of Rahab to stand for You against threats of persecution and criticism. I want strong faith and I want bold courage to serve You and stand for You. Amen.

READ:

Joshua 2:1-24

Day 20

DAVID'S FAITH

How much more do I need to say? It would
take too long to recount the stories of the
faith of Gideon, Barak, Samson, Jephthah,
David, Samuel, and all the prophets.

Hebrews 11:32, NLT

THE faith of David is listed in God's Hall of Fame, which could be titled "God's Hall of Faith." David did so much by faith, yet he is only mentioned by name, without listing any of his accomplishments. Was the author of Hebrews running out of time and space and only listed David by name without recording his many leaps/steps of faith? On the other hand, the Hall of Faith could not be written without including David. Think of his battle with Goliath, his struggles with King Saul, and his many battles over enemy nations. Think of David's establishment of Jerusalem as the capital city, of his preparation to build the temple. Yes, David was a man of faith who took many leaps/steps of faith.

Lord, thank You for David's example of accomplishments
of faith, but more importantly thank You for all his psalms
that teach me the life of faith and the intimacies of fellowship
with You. Give me the faith of David. Amen.

David may be listed only by name in God's Hall of Faith, but his influence and actions are written many places in the New Testament. David's influence for God is noteworthy because it reflects his deep walk with God and faith in God. The fact that David is mentioned only by name in this chapter shows the importance and the influence of David's faith.

Lord, thank You for David and all he did for You and Your work. May I live by his principles and may I enjoy the fellowship David experienced. Amen.

READ:

1 Samuel 17:20-58

Day 21

FAITH HISTORY

By faith these people overthrew kingdoms, ruled with
justice, and received what God had promised them.
They shut the mouths of lions, quenched the flames
of fire, and escaped death by the edge of the sword.
Their weakness was turned to strength. They became
strong in battle and put whole armies to flight.

Hebrews 11:33-34, NLT

IT would be impossible to include all the people of faith in the Old Testament who took significant steps of faith in this chapter of Hebrews. This reference tells us they were many and their faith accomplished a large number of faith experiences—so large they can't be included in this small space. But this summary of Old Testament faith experiences anticipates many New Testament faith experiences. So many have taken a leap/step of faith that it's impossible to list them all. That brings us to you, your family, and members of your church. What have you done in faith? How would God write *your* faith history?

Lord, thank You for all those names included in Scripture
that have made faith leaps/steps. Help me to make my own
leap/step of faith. Lord, You know my weaknesses, but You
also know my convictions; help me—give me faith. Amen.

It would be humanly impossible to include every person in a written record of their leaps/steps of faith. Yet we know God has a book in Heaven (see Malachi 3:16) where these experiences are recorded. What will you see in your record when you get to Heaven? Live for the Lord today, and serve Him so that new additions will be written about you.

Lord, I serve You because of my love and adoration for You. I don't do it to gain merit or a remembrance in Heaven. I serve out of love and appreciation for all You have done for me. Amen.

READ:

Malachi 3:1–4:6

Day 22

EXERCISE YOUR WEAK FAITH

Faith as a mustard seed.

Matthew 17:20

Abraham ... weak in faith.

Romans 14:19

D O you think you have weak faith? Take heart, Jesus said to use what faith you have to do the work of God. Peter was sinking in the waves when he cried out for Jesus to save him. It is then that Jesus said his faith was weak—but it was enough to save him. The Bible describes faith as weak, a grain of mustard seed, and little. The point? If you have just a little faith, use it. God can save you as Peter was saved from drowning. Don't wait till you have strong faith —or big faith; use the faith you have and it will grow. God will recognize and use the small faith you have, but you must trust your weak faith to work for you.

Lord, I have said many times my faith is weak. Forgive me for focusing on my weakness, but I am a sinner. I will attach

my weak faith to You—because You can do the unexpected
(see Philippians 4:13). Amen.

We see weak faith when we first see Abraham. The Bible says, "weak in faith." But through some failures and through some victories, Abraham attained "strong faith" (Romans 4:20). How did it get strong? Abraham exercised the faith he possessed, and it became strong. The same thing happens to weak muscles; when you exercise them, your muscles will grow stronger. Is that what you want God to do for your faith?

Lord, forgive me for focusing on my weak faith. I will focus on You and what You can accomplish. I want You to work Your ministry through my life. Strengthen my faith as I exercise it for ministry and for Your glory. Amen.

READ:

Romans 4:1-25

Day 23

FAITH GROWS

Your faith groweth exceedingly.

2 Thessalonians 1:3, KJV

From faith to faith.

Romans 1:17

DID you see in today's verses that your faith can grow? It can grow stronger (qualitatively), i.e., your daily walk of faith can grow stronger. But also your faith can grow quantitatively; that means you can grow in the use of different expressions of faith. This is using various ways you use faith, i.e., saving faith, justifying faith, indwelling faith, spiritual gifts of faith, and faith-walking. Just think about it: you have many ways to grow faith. But the question is, are you growing more expressions of faith and are you growing in the use/application of each of these expressions of faith? You have faith—that is wonderful! But is it growing in every way possible?

> *Lord, I have not tried to grow my faith. I have just followed You and live what is taught in Scripture. As I have done that, I have had to express my faith in many different ways to do many different things/ministries for You. Thank You*

for growing my faith when I did not realize it was growing.
Amen.

The Christian life is challenging ... active ... and you must grow to meet new challenges every day. You must grow your Bible knowledge, your ministry skills, and your faith. You must grow in every area of life. From time to time you will find yourself focusing on just one area at a time. That is alright. Grow when there are needs and challenges. Grow when you need development and maturity. But eventually, give attention to all areas and grow in Christ to glorify Jesus Christ.

Lord, show me where I need to grow/improve, and I will give my attention there. Guide my growth to glorify both You and the heavenly Father. Amen.

READ:

Colossians 2:1-23

Day 24

DAILY PRAYER

Lord, increase our faith.

Luke 17:5

I S that your daily prayer? It ought to be. Why? Because you can grow your faith larger than it is, and you can grow it daily. Some people grow their faith faster than you, but the question is, are you growing your faith as you should? Some people have stronger faith than you do, but the question is, is your faith as strong as it ought to be? Don't compare your spirituality to others. There will always be someone stronger or weaker than you. Keep your eyes on Jesus's ministry and compare yourself to Him. That way, you will always be challenged to grow in faith—all expressions of faith. Also, you will always keep growing stronger than you were in the past.

> *Lord, forgive me for comparing myself to other believers. Help me keep my eyes on Jesus. He is my standard, and He is the source of my faith. As long as I have Jesus in my heart— controlling my life—I will grow according to His expectations. Amen.*

Technically, our aim is not to strengthen our faith; that is only a byproduct of Christianity. Your aim is to be indwelt by Jesus and let Him control/direct your life. Aim to serve Him with all your heart's

---

devotion and strength. Aim to glorify Jesus in all you do, and finally, aim to worship Him from the bottom of your heart.

Lord, increase my faith, just as You increased the disciples' faith. I want to follow You ... serve You ... advance Your Kingdom ... and worship You because You are the Lord God. Amen.

READ:

Luke 17:1-37

Day 25

FAITH FROM THE SCRIPTURES

Faith cometh by hearing ... the Word of God.

Romans 10:17, KJV

THERE are many ways the Bible can grow your faith. First, make sure you are in places where you hear the reading of the Word of God, but this also includes your personal daily reading of the Bible (see Revelation 1:3). When you read the Bible, you will grow spiritually. Next, go to church and other places where you hear the Word of God (see Revelation 1:3). This seed action of hearing with your ears gives second insight into God's Word. Third, "study to show yourself worthy" (2 Timothy 2:15). When you study the Bible, you bring all your human response to God. The fourth area is memorizing Scripture. Learn the Bible so you can repeat it from memory. "How can a young man cleanse his way? By taking heed according to Your Word" (Psalm 119:9).

Lord, thank You for giving me the Bible to read, study, and memorize. I will hide Your Word in my heart so I can know You better and serve You effectively. Amen.

The first step is to meditate on the Bible. "Thy Word have I hid in my heart, that I might not sin against thee" (Psalm 119:11, KJV). When you hide God's Word in your heart, and you meditate on it, first you put evil thoughts out of your mind. Second, evil thoughts cannot come back in because the Bible is there. But it is more than Bible verses protecting you; it is the Lord Himself living in your mind and heart. He will keep you pure.

Lord, I will hide Your Word in my mind and heart to think about You and worship You. Your Word will keep me thinking about You, serving You, and worshipping You. Amen.

READ:

Psalm 119:1-16

Day 26

JESUS EYES

Looking unto Jesus, the author
and finisher of our faith.

Hebrews 12:1

THE secret of faith-walking is keeping our eyes on Jesus. First, remember that there are many things you will see in life that will distract your eyes from Jesus and will weaken or destroy your faith. Remember that the world, the flesh, and the devil want your attention (see 1 John 2:15-18). It will cause problems when you look at them ... focus on them ... follow them. What you see will determine where you will walk/follow. So don't focus your eyes on evil. Second, there are good things you will see in life, i.e., occupation, marriage, friends, hobbies. Make sure you include Jesus in every area of your life and look at those good things through *Jesus eyes*. Plan to look at things in life as Jesus sees them.

> *Lord, I will fix my eyes on Jesus and follow Him. I will look*
> *at everything in life through Jesus eyes. That way I will best*
> *serve You and please You. Amen.*

Our eyes are the human instruments that tell our minds what to think and our hearts what to like/dislike. Make sure you dedicate your eyes to Jesus and learn to look at life through His eyes. Then you will develop Jesus eyes to guide your every step.

Lord, I yield my eyes to You. Jesus, please live in my heart and look at the world through my eyes. Help me know what is good and what is evil, then give me strength to follow Your direction. Amen.

READ:

Hebrews 12:1-26

Day 27

SEEKING GOD

When You said, "seek ye My face," my heart
said to You, "Your face will I seek."

Psalm 27:8, KJV

WHY must you seek the Lord? For many reasons: protection, guidance, eternal life, answers to prayers, etc. But the psalmist is telling us to seek God, i.e., to be intimate with Him. What does intimacy mean? When you have a need or problem, you get God's help. When you want God's blessing in your work/ministry, you seek His intimacy, or presence. Why seek God? Because the Lord promised to be with you as you walk through the dangers of death's valley (see Psalm 23:4) and He promised to be with you as you serve Him (see Matthew 28:20).

> *Lord, I seek Your presence in my life because I cannot make it by myself. I need Your help and guidance. I want Your protection and blessing. Basically, I need Your presence. I need You! Amen.*

Note that in today's reading, it is God who begins the conversation. God said, "seek My face." How have you done that today? What do you need, and what can God do for you? The Lord invites you to "seek His face." When you do it, you will find His presence, and with it you will find His guidance, His protection, and His promise of eternal life. How do you seek God? In prayer. Wouldn't that be a good thing to do right now?

> *Lord, I seek Your presence in my life. I need You and I want You to walk beside me and indwell me. I want You, my Lord, to walk with me through life today—and always. Amen.*

READ:

Psalm 27:1-14

Day 28

WALKING IN THE LIGHT

If we walk in the light ... the blood of Jesus
Christ ... cleanseth us from all sin.

1 John 1:7, KJV

THE condition is to walk in the light. When you do that, God has promised to cleanse you from all sin. Then the author goes further: "If we confess our sins, He is faithful and just to forgive us our sins and to cleanse us from all unrighteousness" (1 John 1:9). Confession means we acknowledge what we have done and take responsibility for our sins. But it also goes further: we ask God to forgive our sins. When we do that, God forgives our sins and cleanses us from all unrighteousness. How much will God forgive? All unrighteousness! Is that something you want to do now?

Lord, I try to walk in Your light, but I have sinned. Forgive
me ... cleanse me ... accept me back into fellowship with You.
I want to serve You and worship You. Amen.

Because you are a follower of Jesus, you are *light-walking*. You walk in His light, because Jesus said, "I am the light of the world" (John 8:12). When you walk in Jesus's light, you *see* Him: you *see* God's plan for your life, you *see* a needy world, and you *see* what you ought to be doing to serve Him. Yes, you are a *light-walker*. Keep your eyes on Jesus, the light of the world.

Lord, I will walk in Your light, so help me to follow You. I will serve You in Your light, so keep showing me what to do. I will keep worshipping You because You are light; what else can I do? Amen.

READ:

1 John 1:1–2:5

Day 29

MANY EXPRESSIONS OF FAITH

From faith to faith.

Romans 1:17

Oh, you of little faith.

Matthew 14:31

LOOK again at the two verses in today's devotion. They suggest there is more than one expression of faith. First, there is your original *saving faith* (see Ephesians 2:8-9), and then there is daily or continuing faith, called *faith-walking* (see 2 Corinthians 5:11). That suggests faith is foundational to your walk with God. But look at the next expression of your faith. Your faith can be "little," which is another way of saying that your faith can be weak (see Romans 4;19). The opposite of that is strong faith (see Romans 4:20). What does that mean? Give attention to your faith and don't take it for granted. You can strengthen your faith, and that includes strengthening every different expression of faith.

Lord, I will give attention to my faith to strengthen it in every way possible. Also, I will express it in many different ways as I live for You and serve You. Guide me daily and teach me what I need to know to grow in faith and serve by faith. Amen.

Today's lesson challenges you to find each expression of faith so you will be a well-rounded believer who can serve the Lord in as many ways as possible and with all possible strength. But you will also be challenged to grow every experience of faith so you don't have weak faith but strong faith.

Lord, I want to grow as much as possible, in every way possible. Help me as I study faith; send the Holy Spirit to teach me faith as I study the Scriptures to learn faith and to know You better. Amen.

READ:

Romans 4:1-25

Day 30

FAITH TO USE SPIRITUAL GIFTS

Since we have gifts that differ according to the grace
given to us, each of us is to use them accordingly:
if [someone has the gift of] prophecy, [let him
speak a new message from God to His people]
in proportion to the faith possessed; if service, in
the act of serving; or he who teaches, in the act
of teaching; or he who encourages, in the act of
encouragement; he who gives, with generosity;
he who leads, with diligence; he who shows
mercy [in caring for others], with cheerfulness.

Romans 12:6-8, AMP

TODAY'S reading tells us to serve the Lord with the gifts He has given to us. At the center of this passage on serving, Paul added this basis of serving: "in proportion to the faith possessed." Here Paul is suggesting that faith is a spiritual gift, along with the other gifts God has given us. But it seems he is telling us the spiritual gift of faith relates to all other spiritual gifts. As we use the spiritual gifts of prophecy, serving, teaching, giving, leading, showing mercy, we can be effective if we exercise each with our spiritual gift of faith. Do you have these gifts? Do you exercise faith when using them?

Lord, I don't have enough faith; give me more faith to serve You better. And strengthen the faith I already have to continue ministering the walk You have given me. Amen.

The Lord has given you faith to serve Him, and that faith can strengthen each different area of your ministry. So find your gifts and use those that are most effective. Use your faith to make them more effective.

Lord, help me grow my faith to serve You better. I need stronger faith to get started earlier and serve You longer. Lord, I believe; overcome my unbelief. Amen.

READ:

Romans 12:1-21

Day 31

SPIRITUAL GIFTS
FROM GOD

Having then different expressions of faith
according to the gifts that are given to us.

Romans 12:2,5, ELT

GOD has given you the spiritual gift of faith so you can effectively use all the other spiritual gifts He has given you. That means you can grow your spiritual gifts and "desire earnestly the best gifts" (1 Corinthians 13:2). You can grow in the different kinds/expressions of faith, and you can grow in the strength and intensity of each spiritual gift. These gifts will then identify you to other believers in your service to God. "Everyone has his proper gift" (1 Corinthians 7:7). Do you know your various abilities/spiritual gifts that can serve God, and do you use your spiritual gifts/abilities effectively and continually?

> *Lord, I yield all my spiritual gifts/abilities to You. Use them*
> *according to Your will and help me learn to grow my gifts*
> *to be effective in Your ministry. Guide me daily and fill me*
> *with the Holy Spirit. Amen.*

Remember two challenges: First, you can acquire spiritual gifts that you are not presently using; and second, you can grow the ability and effectiveness of each gift so you can do more for God. These additions are not primarily for your benefit; they will help you do more for God and do it effectively. But the end results will be that you will grow in Christ, be more effective, and bring more glory to God.

Lord, give me any spiritual abilities I do not have. May I use it for Your service and glory. Also, Lord, strengthen all the abilities I have, and may I grow my spiritual gifts to please and serve You. Amen.

READ:

1 Corinthians 12:1-13

Day 32

SERVING — ANYWAY, ALL WAYS

Since we have gifts that differ according to
the grace given to us, each of us is to use them
accordingly ... in proportion to the faith possessed.

Romans 12:6

ONE of the first mentioned spiritual gifts is serving other people. We serve others because of Jesus's example of serving others— also because of the heavenly Father's service to all. But our spiritual gift of serving usually has a particular application to a particular plan, to a particular object, people group or person. And when you use them physically or spiritually, do it with the faith God has given you. That means you are motivated by internal faith, are taught by Scripture, and do it for God's glory and to further God's work on Earth.

> *Lord, thank You for the spiritual gift of serving. Guide me*
> *and use my service for growth in others and in Your king-*
> *dom. Help me serve with a willing spirit and make me as*
> *effective as possible. Amen.*

There are many ways to serve, e.g., financially, physically, and in spiritual matters. Ask God to guide you on what to do, how to do it, when, and where. Your service will glorify God and will advance His work on Earth.

Lord, I yield myself to serve You in ways You choose. I begin with pleasing You; then I want to help/benefit others, and I want my service to grow more spiritually. Help me fulfill Your plan for me on Earth. Amen.

READ:

Romans 13:1-4

Day 33

TEACH BY FAITH

*Having then gifts differing according to the grace
that is given us ... let us use it ... in teaching.*

Romans 12:6-7

He [God] ... gave some ... teachers.

Ephesians 4:11

ONE of the spiritual gifts is teaching, i.e., the act of instructing others or another in knowledge, skills, attitudes, and/or spiritual things. That gift of teaching resides, or begins, in mothers who instruct their young, or all of us who were taught by our mothers. The gift of teaching resides in employers who instruct those who work for them. It is a gift that resides in all of us who instruct our friends, family, co-workers, neighbors, and those we serve through our jobs/occupations. No matter who you are or what you do in life, use your spiritual gift of teaching with all your contacts in life. You have both a spiritual gift of teaching and faith; now receive them and use them.

*Lord, help me in all my dealings with others to be a careful
teacher at all times, remembering there are many things I
still need to learn. Teach me so I can teach others. Amen.*

Since we all have the gift of teaching—not just those in the office, classes—let us do these things. First, receive the responsibility from God, and fulfill it as unto the Lord. Second, teach as carefully and truthfully as the Lord Jesus would do if He were in your place. Third, study to be a better teacher in all your responsibilities, and grow in your spiritual walk with God because of your teaching.

Lord, help me be a loving, careful teacher as was Jesus on this earth. Help me grow in knowledge, faith, and skill to teach effectively. Use me to accomplish Your purpose in my life and in the lives of others. Amen.

READ:

1 Peter 2:1-25

Day 34

FAITH-GIVING

God has dealt to each one a measure
of faith ... he who gives.

Romans 12:3,8

G OD has given each believer the privilege of giving back to Him
from our tithes, treasure, and offerings. First, God has given us
the spiritual gift of faith to understand the meaning of money,
how God wants us to use it, and how God wants us to distribute it to
His various areas of worship and service. Then God has given us the spiritual gift of giving. This begins with salvation, because God has given us
eternal life through the gift of His Son, who gave His life for our sins. It
is all about giving: first God gave to us, and now we give to Him through
His church and with our gifts to others in need. How giving are you in
attitude and in service, and in actual gifts?

Lord, help me in all my dealings with others to be a careful
teacher at all times, remembering there are many things I
still need to learn. Teach me so I can teach others. Amen.

When you give everything to God, begin with the tithe to your
local church (see Malachi 3:10), also including gifts as God gives to
you. Remember, when you give all to God, you keep back part for your
life's necessities and to meet your needs. But even that belongs to God,

because all you are and all you have belongs to God. You do everything to Him and for His glory.

> *Lord, once again I yield my life and body to You. Use me for Your glory and Your ministry. I give all my knowledge and skills to Your use. I yield all my possessions, everything, to You. Guide me to use my "things," because they belong to You. I give everything to You; use me. Amen.*

READ:

2 Corinthians 9:1-15

Day 35

MORE FAITH FOR EFFECTIVE MINISTRY

And though I have the gift ... and
understand all knowledge, and mysteries,
and though I have all faith.

1 Corinthians 13:2

God hath dealt the measure of faith ... in teaching.

Romans 12:3,7

PAUL reminds us, "different expressions of faith ... are given us ... according to the gifts that are given us" (Romans 12:2,5, ELT). This means that both faith and our spiritual gifts (abilities) are gifts from God. First God gives you the gift of faith, which is a spiritual understanding of how to know and serve Him. So the spiritual gift of faith helps you use the other natural abilities God has given you. Today's verses talk about the spiritual gift of teaching. Use your faith to guide you as you instruct others about God and how to serve God. So your faith and your ability to teach will be used by God to help others know about God, know how to be saved, know how to serve God, and above all, know how to worship God.

Lord, thank You for both the gift of faith and the gift of teaching. I will use both gifts to help others and to further Your work on Earth. I dedicate these gifts to You; use them abundantly. Amen.

The spiritual gift of faith will enhance your teaching to family, friends, and others. But that gift of faith will also enhance the other spirituals gifts. A few of them are the gifts of prophecy, counseling, encouragement, giving, administration or organization, and evangelism. What are your strongest spiritual gifts? We can all grow by applying faith. How strong is your faith? What are you doing to strengthen your faith?

Lord, I love serving You in many different ways. Give me more faith to serve You better; and expand my faith so I can expand my service to You in areas where I am not presently serving. Amen.

READ:

Romans 12:1-8; Ephesians 4:1-16

Day 36

LACK OF FAITH

*"You don't have enough faith," Jesus told them.
"I tell you the truth, if you had faith even as
small as a mustard seed, you could say to this
mountain, 'Move from here to there,' and it
would move. Nothing would be impossible."*

Matthew 17:20-21, NLT

WHEN Jesus told His disciples they did not have enough
faith, He could have been talking to you or me. Lack of
faith is a common weakness among believers. Yet, we serve
the Lord God of the universe who has power to create all things. And
His laws control the universe. Since God can do anything, and we are
spiritually related to Him, why can't we do more? Jesus has challenged
us to have as much faith as a small mustard seed. Yet our unbelief seems
to control our desires and thinking. It seems our unbelief surely controls our faith. So we must pray like the father said in Scripture: "Lord, I
believe, help my unbelief" (Mark 11:24).

*Lord, I believe You created the universe, and I believe You
have all power, but I am powerless. Increase my faith so I
can pray and trust You to do the powerful things promised
in Scripture. Help me overcome unbelief; help me grow my
faith. Amen.*

When we look at the perfections of God, we see our imperfections. We need to get our eyes off our weakness and get them onto God. We need to know what God can do for us, when He will do it for us; and we need faith to activate God to do it for us. When we honestly and completely know God, we can begin moving barriers by faith.

Lord, I come seeking stronger faith. I have faith to believe You have saved me and will take me to Heaven. I have faith to believe You exist and hear my prayers. Now give me faith to move obstacles to my prayers. Amen.

READ:

Matthew 17:1-21

Day 37

PURIFYING
YOUR FAITH

*... knowing that the testing of your
faith produces patience...*

James 1:3

*That the genuineness of your faith, being much more
precious than gold that perishes, though it is tested by
fire, may be found to praise, honor, and glory at the
revelation of Jesus Christ, whom having not seen you
love. Though now you do not see Him, yet believing,
you rejoice with joy inexpressible and full of glory.*

1 Peter 1:7-8

BECAUSE when you ask for faith, or for more faith, you may
be asking for more trials and testings. Both James (Jesus's half-
brother) and Peter (Jesus's disciple) knew what it was to go
through persecution and troubles. And our persecution is not arbitrary.
Satan uses trouble to discourage us and cause us to quit. But at the same
time, God uses the fires of persecution to purify us, like gold is purified

---

in fire. So, what is going to come out of fiery persecution? Your faith will be purified, as gold has the impurities burned away by heat/fire in the refiner's fire. Are you going through fires of testing now? What have you learned? What is God teaching you? Will the fires get hotter, or have you learned what God is doing for you?

> *Lord, I don't like persecution, and I am embarrassed by persecution. Teach me what You want me to learn. Don't listen to my complaining, and forgive me for fighting against your cleansing work in my life. Teach me; mold me into Your image. Amen.*

When faith is real, it is purified by fires of persecution. If trouble and persecution make you give up, then question your relationship with God. Did you really confess your sins, and did you honestly ask for cleansing from sin? If your faith is real, then persecution is another way to give you assurance of salvation. If your faith is real, then praise God for the opportunity to "suffer with Christ." Remember what He endured for you as He went to the cross to die for your sins.

> *Lord, I thank You for opposition and persecution. While it is not comfortable and I don't like it in the flesh, I praise You for the opportunity to identify with Jesus's sufferings. Thank You for suffering and dying for me. Amen.*

READ:

2 Corinthians 5:1-21

Day 38

FAITH NEEDS
TO GROW (1)

That your faith groweth exceedingly.

2 Thessalonians 1:3, KJV

IT is possible to grow your faith. That is the request Paul prayed for the believers in Thessalonica. And if their faith can grow, so can yours. Here are a few beginning steps. First, grow your knowledge of God and Jesus, then you can trust for more. Next, study the Scriptures to see how God works and when God works. As you begin to understand the way God is working in your world, you can better exercise your faith and it will grow in effectiveness. Also, tie your faith to your prayer ministry. Pray for more faith and for growing faith. Pray about the things or ministry for which you are trusting God. Don't forget to confess your unbelief as sin.

> *Lord, I will begin with the above steps; give me strong faith and give me determination to grow spiritually so I can strengthen my faith. Give me faith eyes to understand Scripture so my faith will be strengthened. Amen.*

The next step to grow faith is taking actual steps of faith. Claim the Scriptures and step out on them. Remember, some begin following God with a leap of faith. It does not have to be a giant step; just begin by taking baby steps of faith. Don't put your emphasis on "baby"—the size of your faith. Put your emphases on faith, i.e., the results of faith.

Lord, I believe every word in the Bible is true. Help me apply every word to my thinking and living. I want to walk by faith. I want to trust You for greater answers and greater effectiveness in ministry. Amen.

READ:

1 Thessalonians 1:1-12

Day 39

FAITH NEEDS
TO GROW (2)

Lord, increase our faith.

Luke 17:5

PRAYER is only one way to increase your faith, but your faith won't grow by prayer alone. You stretch your faith by learning more about God, by mastering what the Scriptures teach about faith, by holy living, and by putting God on the spot when you take a leap/step of faith. But prayer is the place to begin growing your faith. First, pray for God to open your eyes as you study God and the Scriptures. Second, pray to God to grow your faith as you serve Him. Third, pray to be more disciplined in taking up your cross to follow Jesus (see Luke 9:23). To have more faith, you must use the faith you already have, and you must "walk in faith" (2 Corinthians 5:7). Every faith experience will be a foundation to help you take bigger steps of faith in the future. Growing your faith is like growing your Christian life. As you grow in one area, it influences all other areas.

> *Lord, I begin my prayer asking You to grow my faith. Now I ask You to grow every area of my life. Give me faith eyes to learn, faith ears to listen to the Holy Spirit, and a faith heart to obey. Amen.*

Don't forget worship. As you naturally follow the instructions of your growing faith, you will focus your attention on Jesus and worship Him. Then you will open your *worship-eyes* to praise and glorify the Father. When you completely focus on the Father, Son, and Holy Spirit, you cannot help but worship. Then thank Him for all He has done for you. When you do that, your faith will grow.

> *Lord, I come to worship You for the creation of the universe and for my conversion to Jesus Christ. Just as I have grown physically and mentally in life, I want to grow spiritually. Give me faith to obey You better and worship You more. Amen.*

READ:

2 Corinthians 5:1-21

Day 40

GROW YOUR FAITH

God has dealt the measure of faith.

Romans 12:3

THIS verse is a reference to a specific expression of faith, i.e., the spiritual gift of faith. When God gives a believer the spiritual ability to serve Him, God also gives the spirit or gift to use the ability. Paul lists the following spiritual gifts: prophecy, serving, teaching, encouraging, giving, leadership, and showing kindness. This list is not complete in this chapter. Paul adds other spiritual gifts in other places. Examine the list. Do you have all of these gifts? If not, seek them. Are some of your gifts weak (see Romans 14:1)? Then seek to strengthen them.

> *Lord, thank You for the spiritual gifts I know I possess. Help me use them in ministry for You. When one is weak, help me strengthen that gift. When one is not evident in my ministry, help me find it and use it to serve and glorify You. Amen.*

Paul exhorts us, "Having then different expressions of faith, according to the gifts that are given to us" (Romans 12:3,5, ELT). Paul wants you to use as much of the faith you have to be as effective as possible in using your gifts. Let your gift of faith and spiritual gifts work together. Is one weaker than the other? Strengthen it!

Lord, I approach You with the faith I have, asking You to strengthen my faith so I can trust You for great answers to prayer. Help me use my faith to activate all my spiritual gifts. Amen.

READ:

Romans 12:1-21

Day 41

HOW LONG?

Continue in prayer.

Colossians 4:2

Pray without ceasing.

1 Thessalonians 5:17

THE Bible says much about quitting too soon. It also tells you, "Don't give up." Didn't Jesus say, "No man, having put his hand to the plough and looking back is fit for the kingdom of God" (Luke 9:62)? So make a twofold promise to God and yourself. First, promise you will not give up now, or at least not with the next problem or obstacle you face. Promise God you will be faithful to Him for the next second ... minute ... hour. Now give all your strength to keep that promise. Remember, Paul said, "I can do all things through Christ who strengthens me" (Philippians 1:21). Claim that verse and be faithful for the next second ... minute ... hour.

> *Lord, I am human, with temptations to give up, but I will remain faithful to You. I will not give up in the next second ... minute ... or hour. I will be faithful to You ... always! Amen.*

Have you made a commitment to never give up? Have you told God you will be faithful to Him forever? That is a long time. How long? Forever is as long as eternity. God loves you with eternal love, and God will be faithful to you forever. Now let's ask the question again: how long will you remain faithful to God?

Lord, I will be faithful to You for the next second ... minute ... hour. I will be faithful forever. Thank You for Your love that lasts forever—for eternity. Amen.

READ:

John 3:1-36

Day 42

WATCH

Watch and pray, lest you enter into temptation.
The spirit indeed is willing, but the flesh is weak.

Matthew 26:41

ECAUSE our flesh (our human body and inner man) is weak, Jesus told us to "watch and pray." He did not tell us where to look; so which way do you think our Lord meant for us to look? Are we to look inwardly at our old nature that tempts us? Then are we to pray for strength in the inward person? Or did Jesus mean for us to "watch" out for people who will deceive us ... trick us ... tempt us? Are we to keep a sharp eye for anyone who might sneak up on our blind eye and trip us up so that we fall into temptation? Maybe we have to "watch out" for the carnal or fleshly people who will be a bad example to us. Maybe they will try to influence you to quit following Jesus as closely as you do.

Lord, give me spiritual eyes to see my old sinful nature and give me a spiritual mind to resist its temptation. Also, give me spiritual understanding to see when someone else is pulling me away from You. Amen.

Another thing to watch: look out for satan, who will use the glamorous lights of this world to draw you into worldly pleasures. Or satan will use the seductive attraction of money, power, or position to draw you away from Christ. Or satan will use your pride or self-advancement to fulfill your ego hunger.

Lord, give me eyes to see all forms of temptation. Help me see things that will pull me away from You. I need Your wisdom, so please teach me ... guide me ... protect me ... and use me in Your service. Amen.

READ:

2 Corinthians 4:1-18

Day 43

PRAY ... PLAN ... WORK

Lord, increase our faith.

Luke 17:5

HAVE you seen and read the story of the disciples asking Jesus for more faith? What have you done about their question? Have you ever asked God for more faith ... or stronger faith ... or faith to move a mountain (see Mark 11:22-24)? Maybe you don't have greater faith because you have not asked/prayed for increased faith. First, make it a one-time request; ask God to increase your faith daily. Second, make it a daily request so that you ask God to increase your faith every day when you have your devotions. Make the exhortation of James come true: "You have not because you ask not" (James 4:2).

> *Lord, this may be the first time I have asked, but please increase my faith. I ask it now, and I will continue daily asking for faith. Why? Because I need more faith. Amen.*

As you ask for increased faith, study the topic of faith in Scripture to learn more about it. Then write in your prayer journal a project that will stretch your faith. Then plan for that project ... work for that project ... get help for your project. Now pray for God to complete that project.

Lord, give me faith to plan for a project bigger than my faith; then grow my expectations and grow my plans. Finally, grow my faith to trust You for completion of the project. Amen.

READ:

James 4:1-17

Day 44

MORE BIBLE

Faith cometh by hearing ... the Word of God.

Romans 10:13

HOW can you get more faith? One of the answers is to get more of the Bible, because faith comes from Scripture. The more Scripture/Bible you have, the greater your faith. But it's not just head knowledge of the Bible that produces faith. There are some with a PhD in Bible knowledge, and they know Greek and Hebrew, the original languages of the Bible, yet their lives are empty and their ministry is small. They have head knowledge of the Bible, but the teaching of Scripture has not gripped their daily lives, nor has it influenced their feelings/love for God. Their knowledge of the Bible didn't influence their faith.

> *Lord, I want more faith and I pray for it daily. I will study Your Scriptures, the source of faith, and I will apply Scripture to see it work in my life. And I will live the Scriptures so that Christ—the Word of God—will flow through me in faith. Amen.*

The Bible is a supernatural book; it is inspired (in-breathed) by God so that the words of the Bible are the words of Jesus. When I let the Bible control my life, I let Jesus direct my thinking, speaking, and actions. I will learn more of the Bible so that Jesus can be a greater influence in my life.

> *Lord, I memorize Your Word to know exactly what You want me to know. I meditate on Your Word so my mind will be controlled by You. I will live Your Word so You can influence my life, my ministry, and my world. Amen.*

READ:

Psalm 119:1-24

Day 45

STRONGER FAITH
DAY BY DAY

Your faith groweth exceedingly.

2 Thessalonians 1:3, KJV

From faith to faith.

Romans 1:17

YOUR faith is not a solid object like a block of granite. No, your faith is like the body of a baby; it can grow and get stronger, so much more than it presently can do. But a baby cannot do everything that a 21-year-old can do. No! It doesn't have muscle power, or brain power, or the power of determination, nor does it have character to do the right thing, in the right way, at the right time. How can our faith grow? Where does it need to grow? Just like every other living organism, it needs energy to grow. It needs the energy of your growing mind to know and understand faith, which is based on truth and knowledge. And faith needs the wisdom of character to choose wisely and to choose truth each time. Faith needs the total dedication of love, hope, and truth. Your faith must be based on purity.

Lord, give me faith. That is a big request and it will take a lifetime to obtain great faith. But I commit myself to learning faith and living by faith. That is because I commit myself to You. Amen.

When the Bible says "from faith to faith," it does not mean from weak faith to strong faith. No. There are many expressions of faith. There are many ways to use faith as you live for God and serve Him. But to learn all the expressions of faith, you start with growing your faith stronger day by day and year by year—as you look to Jesus and learn from Him.

Lord, I want stronger faith, so I will learn it from Scripture. Then I will pray for stronger faith. I will look to You. Then I will begin exercising what faith I have so it will grow. Amen.

READ:

2 Thessalonians 21:1-12

Day 46

LOOKING TO JESUS GROWS FAITH

*Therefore, we also, since we are surrounded by so
great a cloud of witnesses, let us lay aside every
weight, and the sin which so easily ensnares us, and
let us run with endurance the race that is set before
us, looking unto Jesus, the author and finisher of
our faith, who for the joy that was set before Him
endured the cross, despising the shame, and has
sat down at the right hand of the throne of God.*

Hebrews 12:1-2

AS you run your race in life, keep your eyes on Jesus, because He is the author of your faith. Isn't an author the one who has a message in his head that he writes down for all to see? Jesus saw you from the foundations of time, because He is the Creator of all things (see Colossians 1:17). Since Jesus saw you first, then in time you became a Christian. You saw Jesus in your mind and heart; that is the first act of faith. So seeing Jesus and being seen by Him resulted in your act of faith—your salvation. Now continue to live for Jesus by keeping your eyes on Him as you live for Him ... serve Him ... and bring glory to Him.

Lord, I see You in my mind when I pray to You. I see You in the pages of my Bible when I read Your Word. Now I want to talk to You in prayer and call You to cleanse me ... fill me ... use me ... and guide me in my life. Amen.

This verse tells us Jesus is the finisher of our salvation. Just as He began my salvation before creating the world and died for me on Calvary, He finished my salvation when He announced on the cross, "It is finished" (John 19:30).

Lord, thank You for creating everything in the beginning, and thank You that one day You will finish the task by delivering me to live with You in Heaven. I am looking forward to that event, and I am waiting on You. Amen.

READ:

John 19:23-30; 20:1-31

Day 47

SEEKING GOD
TO GROW

*When You said, "Seek My face," My heart
said to You, "Your face, Lord, I will seek."*

Psalm 27:8

YOU grow your faith by seeking intimacy with God. When the Lord invited you to "seek His face," what did you do? Some turn away; then there are those not interested in growing their faith or learning more about the Lord. A few just come to church once a week to learn a little about God and how to live for Him. But you responded when God said to "seek His face." What did you think and feel and do? When you seek God, it starts in your mind. You made a decision to know God, to know what He has for you, to find out what you have to do for God, and to learn what He wants to show you. Once you decided, then you began looking for God. You can see Him, the Creator of the world, God (see Psalm 19), but you will learn more about Him in the Bible.

Lord, I seek to know You, so I will study Your Word to learn about You. Then I will apply what I know about You to my life to see how You change/transform me. The more You change my life, the more I learn about You, and I love You more. Amen.

When I began seeking God, I knew very little about Him, and I did not know what He could do, especially do for me. I have found that the more I seek God, the more He shows me Himself. Then every time I learn some new truth about God, I want to seek more and find more and know more about Him.

Lord, I will seek You every day—early in the morning. Reveal Yourself to me through the pages of Scripture. Help me to learn more about You and become more like You; and guide me as I continue to seek You. Amen.

READ:

Psalm 27:1-14

Day 48

BY OBEDIENCE
AND EXERCISE

If you love Me, keep My commandments.

John 14:15

The priests were obedient to the faith.

Acts 6:7

OUR faith will grow when we obey the Word of God, because faith comes from God's Word (see Romans 10:13). But each time we obey the Word of God, we energize our faith; and constantly exercising our muscles will strengthen them, just as constantly exercising our faith will give us *growing faith*. And that will lead to *strong faith*. Jesus told His disciples that their obedience in reading the Bible reflected their love to the heavenly Father. And we could add, obedience reflected their faith. Look at the priests who were saved in the early church; they had obedient faith. Remember, these same priests represented the ones who were responsible for the death of Jesus. So these priests, like you and all others, can demonstrate faith in Jesus by obedience to His Word.

Lord, I love Your Word. I will read it, memorize it, and obey it. That is a reflection of my faith in You. Thank You for Scripture that builds up my faith and challenges me to greater faith. I love Your Bible, which is called "the Word of faith" (Acts 4:31; 6:2). Amen.

Did you know the Bible calls itself "the Word of faith" (Romans 10:8)? So, when you memorize the words of the Bible, you digest faith. When you obey the Bible, you exercise your faith. When you meditate on the words of Scripture, your faith is rooted and grounded in the Word of God.

Lord, I want more faith, so I will learn the Bible. Then when I want more faith than that, I will obey the Bible. When I want to live by faith, I will live according to the Bible. Amen.

READ:

Romans 10:1-18

Day 49

GRATITUDE GROWS FAITH

So, walk in Him ... established in the
faith ... with thanksgiving.

Colossians 2:6-7

HAVE you ever thought that gratitude—being thankful—could grow your faith? Technically, faith is based on the Word of God (see Romans 10:13), and you exercise faith by looking to Jesus (see Hebrews 12:2). But when you show gratitude to other people for their good works and honest intentions, you are actually displaying love, support, and you build up the other person. Your actions are reflecting your faith in God and His expectations of you. Anytime you are pleasing God, your actions are faith-based. "Without faith it is impossible to please Him" (Hebrews 11:6). When you show genuine gratitude to others, you are doing what God would do.

> *Lord, thank You for salvation and for those who led me to Christ. Thank You for my church, my fellow believers, and my neighbors. Thank You for my parents, family, and relatives. I would not be what I am without them. Amen.*

We cannot make it through life without help from all who give us aid, both paid and unpaid. We should be thankful for anything and all things that someone does for us. It is common decency when someone does anything for you; it is your obligation to accept it, recognize it, and appreciate it. It's faith's response to what God expects of you.

Lord, forgive me for my selfishness and ignorance. I appreciate any and all things done for me. Help me always to show gratitude. I am grateful You saved me, forgave my sins, and are preparing a home for me in Heaven. Amen.

READ:

John 14:1-31

PART THREE

FAITH
WALKING
with
JESUS

LESSONS

Lesson 1:

GETTING BIGGER FAITH

A. INTRODUCTION: FAITH, THE SOURCE

1. Jerry Falwell, a freshman at Baptist Bible College, 195"You will never build a class …" Prayed from 1:00 p.m. to 5:00 p.m. daily. Built his Sunday school class from 1 to 53; had over 100 on big attendance days. **Faith and works**.

2. Jerry Falwell: "I don't have great faith … I have a **great God**!"

3. First meeting, Falwell and Towns set a goal of 100,000 students at Liberty. **Visionary faith**.

4. In 1978, needed $5 million for 7 dorms. "God, You have got a lot of money and I need some." **Five months later, occupied dorms**.

5. In 1992, faced bankruptcy; needed $104 million. Fasted 40 days—twice. "I don't mind dying … you have to die spiritually to get God's life and **die to self** to get God's answer." A.L. Williams sent $52 million by courier. Today, $1.2 billion.

B. FAITH HAS MANY SIZES

1. **Mountain-moving** faith. "Then Jesus said to the disciples, 'Have faith in God. I tell you the truth, you can say to this mountain, May you be lifted up and thrown into the sea, and it will happen. But you must really believe it will happen and have no doubt in your heart'" (Mark 11:22-23, NLT).

2. **Little** faith. "Why do you have so little faith?" (Matthew 6:30).

3. Great faith. "Jesus ... marveled ... I have not found such great faith, not even in Israel!" (Matthew 8:10).

4. Weak faith. "Abraham ... who against hope ... weak faith" (Romans 4:16,18-19).

5. **Strong** in faith. "Did not waver at the promise of God ... but was strengthened in faith" (Romans 4:20).

6. Faith can **grow**. "Increase our faith" (Luke 17:5).

7. Faith can be great. "Then Jesus answered ... 'Oh woman, great is your faith!'" (Matthew 15:28).

8. Faith can fail. "I have prayed ... faith fail not" (Luke 22:32).

9. **Abundant** faith. "Rich in faith" (James 2:5).

10. **Healing** faith. "Faith hath made thee whole" (Mark 5:2, KJV).

11. **Small faith**. "Faith as a grain of mustard seed" (Matthew 17:20).

12. No faith. "You have not faith" (Mark 4:40).

C. DEFINITION OF FAITH

1. "Faith" is *pistis* in the Greek perfect tense and is a non-verb hybrid: "to have belief." The verb *pisteuo* is action, i.e., **belief**, trust, rely on, act on, receive, accept, or rest on. The object of your faith must motivate you to respond/act, either **outwardly or inwardly**.

2. Faith is validated by the **authenticity** of its object, i.e., the thing, action, or person into which/where you have faith.

3. Therefore, it is not faith that heals; **it is God**. It is not faith that sends millions of dollars; it is God.

4. Faith is a road God uses to get you there. Faith is a **tool** God uses to fix your problem. Faith is the medicine God uses to heal.

5. "Now faith is the substance of things hoped for, the evidence of things not seen" (Hebrews 11:1, KJV). "Faith is the title deed that gives us access to things we hope for; it is the conviction that they exist" (Hebrews 11:1, ELT).

6. Your **prayer** for this series: "Lord, increase our faith" (Luke 17:5).

7. Your assignment: look up and study the word "**faith**."

8. Your application: ask God to lead you to take a step/leap of faith; **then do it**.

Lesson 1:

GETTING BIGGER FAITH

A. INTRODUCTION: FAITH, THE SOURCE

1. Jerry Falwell, a freshman at Baptist Bible College, 195 "You will
    never build a class ..." Prayed from 1:00 p.m. to 5:00 p.m. daily.
    Built his Sunday school class from 1 to 53; had over 100 on big
    attendance days. _____ .

2. Jerry Falwell: "I don't have great faith ... I have a
    _____ !"

3. First meeting, Falwell and Towns set a goal of 100,000 students at
    Liberty. _____ .

4. In 1978, needed $5 million for 7 dorms. "God, You have got a lot
    of money and I need some."

    _____ .

5. In 1992, faced bankruptcy; needed $104 million. Fasted 40
    days—twice. "I don't mind dying ... you have to die spiritually to
    get God's life and _____ to get God's answer." A.L.
    Williams sent $52 million by courier. Today, $1.2 billion.

B. FAITH HAS MANY SIZES

1. _____ faith. "Then Jesus said to the disciples, 'Have faith in God. I tell you the truth, you can say to this mountain, May you be lifted up and thrown into the sea, and it will happen. But you must really believe it will happen and have no doubt in your heart'" (Mark 11:22-23, NLT).

2. _____ faith. "Why do you have so little faith?" (Matthew 6:30).

3. Great faith. "Jesus ... marveled ... I have not found such great faith, not even in Israel!" (Matthew 8:10).

4. Weak faith. "Abraham ... who against hope ... weak faith" (Romans 4:16,18-19).

5. _____ in faith. "Did not waver at the promise of God ... but was strengthened in faith" (Romans 4:20).

6. Faith can _____ . "Increase our faith" (Luke 17:5).

7. Faith can be great. "Then Jesus answered ... 'Oh woman, great is your faith!'" (Matthew 15:28).

8. Faith can fail. "I have prayed ... faith fail not" (Luke 22:32).

9. _____ faith. "Rich in faith" (James 2:5).

10. _____ faith. "Faith hath made thee whole" (Mark 5:2, KJV).

11. _____ . "Faith as a grain of mustard seed" (Matthew 17:20).

12. No faith. "You have not faith" (Mark 4:40).

C. DEFINITION OF FAITH

1. "Faith" is *pistis* in the Greek perfect tense and is a non-verb hybrid: "to have belief." The verb *pisteuo* is action, i.e., _____ , trust, rely on, act on, receive, accept, or rest on. The object of your faith must motivate you to respond/act, either _____ .

2. Faith is validated by the _____ of its object, i.e., the thing, action, or person into which/where you have faith.

3. Therefore, it is not faith that heals; _____ . It is not faith that sends millions of dollars; it is God.

4. Faith is a road God uses to get you there. Faith is a _____ God uses to fix your problem. Faith is the medicine God uses to heal.

5. "Now faith is the substance of things hoped for, the evidence of things not seen" (Hebrews 11:1, KJV). "Faith is the title deed that gives us access to things we hope for; it is the conviction that they exist" (Hebrews 11:1, ELT).

6. Your _____ for this series: "Lord, increase our faith" (Luke 17:5).

7. Your assignment: look up and study the word "_____."

8. Your application: ask God to lead you to take a step/leap of faith; _____ .

Lesson 2:

SIX EXPRESSIONS OF FAITH IN SCRIPTURE

INTRODUCTION: FAITH THAT PLEASES GOD

1. The irreducible **minimum:** "But without faith it is impossible to please Him, for he who comes to God must believe that He is, and that He is a rewarder of those who diligently seek Him" (Hebrews 11:6).

   a. The question: "**Do I please God**?"

   b. What does "diligently" mean? **Wholeheartedly**.

2. What does "from faith to faith" mean (Romans 1:17)?

   a. Grow in the **intensity** of faith, i.e., from a 5 to a 10.

   b. Grow in **time**, i.e., from Old Testament faith to New Testament faith.

   c. Grow in **focus** of faith, i.e., from self to others (see 1 Corinthians 13:2).

   d. Grow from **natural** faith to biblical faith.

   e. Grow in six different **expressions** of faith.

FIRST: THE STATEMENT OF FAITH (CONTENT OF BELIEF)

1. This faith is not what you exercise; it is **absolute truth**.

2. Used with an article, i.e., **positively**: "contend for the faith" (Jude 3).

3. Used **negatively**: "depart from the faith" (1 Timothy 4:1), "denied the faith" (1 Timothy 5:8), "erred from the faith" (1 Timothy 6:10,21), "disapproved concerning the faith" (2 Timothy 3:8).

4. What **pleases** God? "I have kept the faith" (2 Timothy 4:7).

5. Why is *faith* imperative?

    a. **Life** (John 6:68; Hebrews 4:12; 2 Timothy 3:16)

    b. **Born again** (James 1:18; 1 Peter 1:23)

    c. **Personal** faith (Romans 10:17)

SECOND: SAVING FAITH

1. Doorway **to heaven**. "For by grace are you saved through faith" (Ephesians 2:8).

2. Both **easy and difficult**.

3. It is not just to believe in doctrines; it is to believe **in a person**.

4. Saving faith involves the total person, not just the head.

    a. **Intellect**. "These are written that you may believe" (John 20:31).

    b. **Emotion**. "Love the Lord thy God with all thy heart" (Matthew 22:37).

    c. **Will**. "Obeyed from the heart" (Romans 6:17).

THIRD: JUSTIFYING FAITH

1. This is not what you do but what you get, i.e., **non-experiential**.

2. You stand perfect before God. "Being justified by faith, we have peace with God through our Lord Jesus Christ" (Romans 5:1).

3. Abraham was the **first**. "He [Abraham] believed in the Lord; and He [God] counted it to him [Abraham] for righteousness" (Genesis 15:6).

4. You are **declared**—not made—righteousness. "As perfect as God's Son." "God made Him [Christ] to be sin for us [first step of transference] ... that we might be made the righteousness of God [second step of transference] in Him" (2 Corinthians 5:21).

FOURTH: INDWELLING FAITH

1. This is **experiential** faith that comes from God when He takes over.

2. We need faith **greater** than our own. "Have faith in God" (Mark 11:22). *Pisteuo theuo* means "have God's faith."

3. Old Testament foundation. "The just shall live by faith" (Hebrews 10:38).

4. We must **yield to Christ**. "I live by the faith of the Son of God" (Galatians 2:20), "by the faith of Jesus Christ" (Galatians 2:16).

5. To activate your indwelling faith, don't hold on harder, but **let go**.

FIFTH: LIVING BY FAITH

1. Many wrongly think it's just **trusting God for money**, i.e., faith institutions.

2. Faith—the only way. "The just shall live by faith" (Hebrews 10:38).

   a. Romans—**justified ones**

   b. Galatians—**live**

   c. Hebrews—**faith**

3. Living by the **principles** of Scripture. "We walk by faith, not by sight" (2 Corinthians 5:7).

SIXTH: THE GIFT OF FAITH: A SPIRITUAL GIFT

1. We receive the gift of faith (see Romans 12:3,6), which is the ability to **serve God** in a powerful and spiritual way.

2. Called **mountain-moving** faith. "If you have faith as a mustard seed, you will say to this mountain, 'Move from here to there,' and it will move" (Matthew 17:20).

3. Not "name it, claim it" faith.

4. Spiritual gifts or talents have different qualities of **usefulness**.

   a. In the parable of the talents, each got a **different amount**.

   b. Gifts can **grow**. "But earnestly desire the best gifts" (1 Corinthians 12:31).

CONCLUSION

1. Ground yourself in **all faiths**. "Though I have all faith" (1 Corinthians 13:2).

2. Begin **where you are**.

3. Plant and **grow** your faith. "Mustard seed" (Matthew 17:20).

Lesson 2:

QUESTIONS

SIX EXPRESSIONS OF FAITH IN SCRIPTURE

INTRODUCTION: FAITH THAT PLEASES GOD

1. The irreducible _____ : "But without faith it is impossible to please Him, for he who comes to God must believe that He is, and that He is a rewarder of those who diligently seek Him" (Hebrews 11:6).

   a. The question: " _____ ?"

   b. What does "diligently" mean? _____ .

2. What does "from faith to faith" mean (Romans 1:17)?

   a. Grow in the _____ of faith, i.e., from a 5 to a 10.

   b. Grow in _____ , i.e., from Old Testament faith to New Testament faith.

   c. Grow in _____ of faith, i.e., from self to others (see 1 Corinthians 13:2).

   d. Grow from _____ faith to biblical faith.

   e. Grow in six different _____ of faith.

FIRST: THE STATEMENT OF FAITH (CONTENT OF BELIEF)

1. This faith is not what you exercise; it is _____ .

2. Used with an article, i.e., _____ : "contend for the faith" (Jude 3).

3. Used _____ : "depart from the faith" (1 Timothy 4:1), "denied the faith" (1 Timothy 5:8), "erred from the faith" (1 Timothy 6:10,21), "disapproved concerning the faith" (2 Timothy 3:8).

4. What _____ God? "I have kept the faith" (2 Timothy 4:7).

5. Why is *faith* imperative?

   a. _____ (John 6:68; Hebrews 4:12; 2 Timothy 3:16)

   b. _____ (James 1:18; 1 Peter 1:23)

   c. _____ faith (Romans 10:17)

SECOND: SAVING FAITH

1. Doorway _____ . "For by grace are you saved through faith" (Ephesians 2:8).

2. Both _____ .

3. It is not just to believe in doctrines; it is to believe _____ .

4. Saving faith involves the total person, not just the head.

   a. _____ . "These are written that you may believe" (John 20:31).

   b. _____ . "Love the Lord thy God with all thy heart" (Matthew 22:37).

   c. _____ . "Obeyed from the heart" (Romans 6:17).

THIRD: JUSTIFYING FAITH

1. This is not what you do but what you get, i.e.,

   _____ .

2. You stand perfect before God. "Being justified by faith, we have
   peace with God through our Lord Jesus Christ" (Romans 5:1).

3. Abraham was the _____ . "He [Abraham] believed
   in the Lord; and He [God] counted it to him [Abraham] for
   righteousness" (Genesis 15:6).

4. You are _____ —not made—righteousness.
   "As perfect as God's Son." "God made Him [Christ] to be sin
   for us [first step of transference] ... that we might be made the
   righteousness of God [second step of transference] in Him" (2
   Corinthians 5:21).

FOURTH: INDWELLING FAITH

1. This is _____ faith that comes from God when He takes over.

2. We need faith _____ than our own. "Have faith in God" (Mark 11:22). *Pisteuo theuo* means "have God's faith."

3. Old Testament foundation. "The just shall live by faith" (Hebrews 10:38).

4. We must _____ . "I live by the faith of the Son of God" (Galatians 2:20), "by the faith of Jesus Christ" (Galatians 2:16).

5. To activate your indwelling faith, don't hold on harder, but _____ .

FIFTH: LIVING BY FAITH

1. Many wrongly think it's just _____ , i.e., faith institutions.

2. Faith—the only way. "The just shall live by faith" (Hebrews 10:38).

   a. Romans— _____

   b. Galatians— _____

   c. Hebrews— _____

3. Living by the _____ of Scripture. "We walk by faith, not by sight" (2 Corinthians 5:7).

SIXTH: THE GIFT OF FAITH: A SPIRITUAL GIFT

1. We receive the gift of faith (see Romans 12:3,6), which is the ability to _____ in a powerful and spiritual way.

2. Called _____ faith. "If you have faith as a mustard seed, you will say to this mountain, 'Move from here to there,' and it will move" (Matthew 17:20).

3. Not "name it, claim it" faith.

4. Spiritual gifts or talents have different qualities of _____ .

    a. In the parable of the talents, each got a _____ .

    b. Gifts can _____ . "But earnestly desire the best gifts" (1 Corinthians 12:31).

CONCLUSION

1. Ground yourself in _____ . "Though I have all faith" (1 Corinthians 13:2).

2. Begin _____ _____ .

3. Plant and _____ your faith. "Mustard seed" (Matthew 17:20).

Lesson 3:

A LEAP OF FAITH

A. INTRODUCTION

1. Faith is __relationship__. "But without faith it is impossible to please Him, for he who comes to God must believe that He is" (Hebrews 11:6).

2. Jerry Falwell said, "Faith is stepping out into the darkness, the __unknown__."

   a. Not __knowing__. "But Abraham ... went out, not knowing where he was going" (Hebrews 11:8).

   b. Not __experienced__. "Faith is ... the evidence of things *not* seen" (Hebrews 11:1).

   c. A leap into the dark to __make it happen__. "Noah ... divinely warned of things not yet seen" (Hebrews 11:7).

3. Many say faith is not a leap into darkness but into light, <u>**stepping into the promise of God**</u>.

   a. Faith is <u>**obedience**</u> to God's call. "Abraham obeyed when he was called" (Hebrews 11:9).

   b. Faith is <u>**claiming a promise**</u>. "Sarah ... judged Him faithful who had promised" (Hebrews 11:11).

   c. Faith acts on <u>**God's Word**</u>. "Abraham ... offered up Isaac ... who had received the promise" (Hebrews 11:17).

4. Faith doesn't always get what it claims.

   a. <u>**Timing**</u>. "These all died in faith, not having received the promise" (Hebrews 11:13).

   b. God has a <u>**different purpose**</u>. "By faith ... others were tortured, not accepting deliverance" (Hebrews 11:31,35). "By faith ... still others had trial of mockings and scourgings, yes, and of chains and imprisonment" (Hebrews 11:36).

   c. Some were <u>**not healed**</u>. "I pleaded with the Lord three times that it might depart from me" (2 Corinthians 12:8).

B. HOW TO LEAP

Definition: "To spring free, as from the ground; to jump over a fence; to pass abruptly from one state to another; to act precipitately."

1. Usually, to leap over an **obstacle or barrier**. "Whoever says to this mountain, 'Be removed and be cast into the sea,' and does not doubt in his heart, but believes ... he will have whatever he says" (Mark 11:23).

2. Usually, to step over your **inner obstacles**. Abraham: "And being not weak in faith ... he staggered not at the promises of God" (Romans 4:19-20).

    a. Fear of harm or **embarrassment**

    b. Loss of security or **things**

    c. Ignorance

    d. **Doubt** or unbelief

3. Ask if you really want to take this leap.

    a. Is it for **God**?

    b. Is it for **self**?

4. The bigger the leap, the more energy needed to clear an obstacle.

    a. **Time** in prayer and planning.

    b. Support from **others**.

    c. Knowledge.

5. You must be **committed** to the leap.

    a. Can't go back, e.g., Abraham, Moses, Joshua.

    b. Can't change **strategies** when halfway there.

6. **Consider** where you will land and where you will be.

    a. Do you really want this **victory**?

    b. What will you do when you get there?

7. Don't expend so much energy on the leap that you can't live when **you get the victory**.

8. Some leaps must be taken **in spite** of fears and obstacles.

    a. Imperative for the work or **reputation of God**.

    b. Imperative for **you**.

9. Some leaps are so dangerous you might not survive.

    a. What will happen to **others**?

    b. What will happen to **the work**?

    c. What will happen to **you**?

C. THE LEAP (ACT) OF FAITH

1. **Intimacy.** "Enoch walked with God, and he was not, for God took him" (Genesis 5:24).

2. **Built an ark.** "By faith Noah ... prepared an ark" (Hebrews 11:7).

3. **Left security.** "By faith Abraham ... went out not knowing where he was going" (Hebrews 11:8).

4. **Blessed sons.** "By faith Isaac blessed" (Hebrews 11:20).

5. **Planned return to land.** "By faith Joseph ... gave instructions concerning his bones" (Hebrews 11:22).

6. **Separation.** "By faith Moses ... choosing ... to suffer affliction" (Hebrews 11:25).

7. **Protected God's servants.** "By faith Rahab ... received the spies in peace" (Hebrews 11:31).

8. **Attacked giant.** "By faith ... David" (Hebrews 11:31-32).

Lesson 3:

QUESTIONS

A LEAP OF FAITH

A. INTRODUCTION

1. Faith is _____ . "But without faith it is impossible to please Him, for he who comes to God must believe that He is" (Hebrews 11:6).

2. Jerry Falwell said, "Faith is stepping out into the darkness, the _____ ."

   a. Not _____ . "But Abraham ... went out, not knowing where he was going" (Hebrews 11:8).

   b. Not _____ . "Faith is ... the evidence of things *not* seen" (Hebrews 11:1).

   c. A leap into the dark to _____ . "Noah ... divinely warned of things not yet seen" (Hebrews 11:7).

3. Many say faith is not a leap into darkness but into light,

    _____ .

    a. Faith is _____ to God's call. "Abraham obeyed when he was called" (Hebrews 11:9).

    b. Faith is _____ . "Sarah ... judged Him faithful who had promised" (Hebrews 11:11).

    c. Faith acts on _____ . "Abraham ... offered up Isaac ... who had received the promise" (Hebrews 11:17).

4. Faith doesn't always get what it claims.

    a. _____ . "These all died in faith, not having received the promise" (Hebrews 11:13).

    b. God has a _____ . "By faith ... others were tortured, not accepting deliverance" (Hebrews 11:31,35). "By faith ... still others had trial of mockings and scourgings, yes, and of chains and imprisonment" (Hebrews 11:36).

    c. Some were _____ . "I pleaded with the Lord three times that it might depart from me" (2 Corinthians 12:8).

B. HOW TO LEAP

Definition: "To spring free, as from the ground; to jump over a fence; to pass abruptly from one state to another; to act precipitately."

1. Usually, to leap over an _____.
    "Whoever says to this mountain, 'Be removed and be cast into the sea,' and does not doubt in his heart, but believes ... he will have whatever he says" (Mark 11:23).

2. Usually, to step over your _____.
    Abraham: "And being not weak in faith ... he staggered not at the promises of God" (Romans 4:19-20).

    a. Fear of harm or _____

    b. Loss of security or _____

    c. Ignorance

    d. _____ or unbelief

3. Ask if you really want to take this leap.

    a. Is it for _____ ?

    b. Is it for _____ ?

4. The bigger the leap, the more energy needed to clear an obstacle.

    a. _____ in prayer and planning.

    b. Support from _____ .

    c. Knowledge.

5. You must be _____ to the leap.

    a. Can't go back, e.g., Abraham, Moses, Joshua.

    b. Can't change _____ when halfway there.

6. _____ where you will land and where you will be.

    a. Do you really want this _____ ?

    b. What will you do when you get there?

7. Don't expend so much energy on the leap that you can't live when _____ .

8. Some leaps must be taken _____ of fears and obstacles.

    a. Imperative for the work or _____ .

    b. Imperative for _____ .

9. Some leaps are so dangerous you might not survive.

    a. What will happen to _____ ?

    b. What will happen to _____ ?

    c. What will happen to _____ ?

C. THE LEAP (ACT) OF FAITH

1. _____ . "Enoch walked with God, and he was not, for God took him" (Genesis 5:24).

2. _____ . "By faith Noah ... prepared an ark" (Hebrews 11:7).

3. _____ . "By faith Abraham ... went out not knowing where he was going" (Hebrews 11:8).

4. _____ . "By faith Isaac blessed" (Hebrews 11:20).

5. _____ . "By faith Joseph ... gave instructions concerning his bones" (Hebrews 11:22).

6. _____ . "By faith Moses ... choosing ... to suffer affliction" (Hebrews 11:25).

7. _____ . "By faith Rahab ... received the spies in peace" (Hebrews 11:31).

8. _____ . "By faith ... David" (Hebrews 11:31-32).

Lesson 4:

ANSWER KEY

IT TAKES TWO
WINGS TO FLY

A. INTRODUCTION

1. Only faith in Christ saves us. "Believe on the Lord Jesus Christ and you will be saved" (Acts 16:31).

   a. Faith is turning to God from idols (see 1 Thessalonians 1:9), which is **repentance**.

      You can't be saved by repentance **alone**.

      You can't be saved without **repentance**.

   b. Peter preached "repent" (Acts 2:38); **Paul** preached "repent" (Acts 17:20; 26:20).

2. After the first wing, salvation, the second wing is **faith-walking**. "We walk by faith, not by sight" (2 Corinthians 5:7).

3. Second wing, **obedience**, prayer, and using principles for God and practical methods.

4. The **division of labor**. God does what only God can do; we do what only man can do. "We are workmen together with God" (1 Corinthians 3:9; 2 Corinthians 6:1).

5. Review. Faith is **relationship-walking with God**. "Without faith it is impossible to please Him, for he who comes to God must believe that He is, and that He is a rewarder of those who diligently seek Him" (Hebrews 11:6).

B. JAMES 2:14-20,26
EXPANDED AND APPLIED

"How effectively can the Christian fly who has one wing of faith but not the natural wing of human effort? Can his faith wing make him fly? If the [one-winged believer] sees a needy Christian and only blesses him in faith, has he done any good? No, his Christian friend is still needy. So a believer with only a faith wing, without a practical wing, can't fly. A believer can't say, 'I have [faith Christianity] but you only have [practical Christianity]. If they first tried to show faith without practical actions, they will not get off the ground. If you have only a faith wing and believe in God, what good is that? The demons also believe in one God, but they at least tremble. You are dumb if you think faith without being practical will work. As the body without the spirit is dead, so your faith is dead if it doesn't have both faith and practical application."

Conclusion: A bird with one wing will never fly off the ground; and if it loses a wing while flying, **it will crash**.

1. Your works are empty without **faith**. "Faith without works is dead" (v. 17).

2. Your faith won't fly without **works** (see v. 20).

3. **You need both**. It takes your works to manifest your faith (see v. 26).

4. Faith that flies must have **God's life**, God's presence, and God's blessing.

5. Practical works make your faith **flyable**. Your faith won't fly until your actions back up your desires.

6. Application

   a. You pray best for **money** when you work hard for a raise, promotion, or commission. The Old Testament Jews didn't only pray for financial prosperity; they also worked hard.

   b. You pray best for **conversions** when you share the gospel, invite people to hear the gospel, and evangelistic visitation.

   c. You pray best for **church growth** when you visit, invite, advertise, plan for visitors, and work for new members.

   d. You can't pray for the church attendance **to grow** if you don't have parking, pews, space, prayers, etc.

C. HOW FAITH AND WORKS COME TOGETHER

1. Commit yourself to **practical ministry** to exercise your faith.

2. Take a leap of faith to let God work when you are willing to also work.

3. If you begin by faith, make sure you **continue in faith**.

4. It will never work if you do half the work and depend on God to do the **other half**.

5. The division of labor: You work as though it **all depends on you**. You trust God as though it **all depends on Him**.

6. You work with God from **beginning to end**.

7. By faith follow a **burden** God gives you.

8. By faith follow the **dream** God gives you.

9. By faith **saturate** yourself in the Bible.

    a. Bible **command**

    b. Bible **principles**

    c. Bible **life**

    d. God **speaks** to you through Scripture.

10. By faith saturate your work with prayer.

    a. Seek His **presence**.

    b. Seek His **will/plan**.

    c. Seek His **priorities**.

    d. **Intercession**

Lesson 4:

QUESTIONS

IT TAKES TWO WINGS TO FLY

A. INTRODUCTION

1. Only faith in Christ saves us. "Believe on the Lord Jesus Christ and you will be saved" (Acts 16:31).

   a. Faith is turning to God from idols (see 1 Thessalonians 1:9), which is _____ .

      You can't be saved by repentance _____ .

      You can't be saved without _____ .

   b. Peter preached "repent" (Acts 2:38); _____ preached "repent" (Acts 17:20; 26:20).

2. After the first wing, salvation, the second wing is _____ . "We walk by faith, not by sight" (2 Corinthians 5:7).

3. Second wing, _____ , prayer, and using principles for God and practical methods.

4. The _____ . God does what only God can do; we do what only man can do. "We are workmen together with God" (1 Corinthians 3:9; 2 Corinthians 6:1).

5. Review. Faith is _____ .
    "Without faith it is impossible to please Him, for he who comes
    to God must believe that He is, and that He is a rewarder of those
    who diligently seek Him" (Hebrews 11:6).

B. JAMES 2:14-20,26
EXPANDED AND APPLIED

"How effectively can the Christian fly who has one wing of faith
but not the natural wing of human effort? Can his faith wing
make him fly? If the [one-winged believer] sees a needy Christian and only blesses him in faith, has he done any good? No,
his Christian friend is still needy. So a believer with only a faith
wing, without a practical wing, can't fly. A believer can't say, 'I
have [faith Christianity] but you only have [practical Christi-
anity]. If they first tried to show faith without practical actions,
they will not get off the ground. If you have only a faith wing
and believe in God, what good is that? The demons also believe
in one God, but they at least tremble. You are dumb if you think
faith without being practical will work. As the body without the
spirit is dead, so your faith is dead if it doesn't have both faith
and practical application."

Conclusion: A bird with one wing will never fly off the ground;
and if it loses a wing while flying, _____ .

1. Your works are empty without _____ . "Faith
    without works is dead" (v. 17).

2. Your faith won't fly without _____ (see v. 20).

3. _____ . It takes your works to manifest your faith (see v. 26).

4. Faith that flies must have _____ , God's presence, and God's blessing.

5. Practical works make your faith _____ . Your faith won't fly until your actions back up your desires.

6. Application

   a. You pray best for _____ when you work hard for a raise, promotion, or commission. The Old Testament Jews didn't only pray for financial prosperity; they also worked hard.

   b. You pray best for _____ when you share the gospel, invite people to hear the gospel, and evangelistic visitation.

   c. You pray best for _____ when you visit, invite, advertise, plan for visitors, and work for new members.

   d. You can't pray for the church attendance _____ if you don't have parking, pews, space, prayers, etc.

C. HOW FAITH AND WORKS COME TOGETHER

1. Commit yourself to _____ to exercise your faith.

2. Take a leap of faith to let God work when you are willing to also work.

3. If you begin by faith, make sure you _____ .

4. It will never work if you do half the work and depend on God to do the _____ .

5. The division of labor: You work as though it _____ . You trust God as though it _____ .

6. You work with God from _____ .

7. By faith follow a _____ God gives you.

8. By faith follow the _____ God gives you.

9. By faith _____ yourself in the Bible.

   a. Bible _____

   b. Bible _____

   c. Bible _____

   d. God _____ to you through Scripture.

10. By faith saturate your work with prayer.

   a. Seek His _____ .

   b. Seek His _____ .

   c. Seek His _____ .

Lesson 5:

ANSWER KEY

FAITH TO USE SPIRITUAL GIFTS

A. MANY PURPOSED FOR FAITH

1. Get more faith. "From faith to faith" (Romans 1:17).

   a. **Intensity**: you get more faith.

   b. **Variety**: you get different kinds of faith.

2. When faith is **not enough**: "Oh, you of little faith" (Matthew 14:31).

3. When faith is **unable**: "Weak in faith" (Romans 14:1).

4. Most believers have faith for a few tasks, but not **all have faith for all tasks**.

B. FAITH ACCORDING TO OUR SPIRITUAL GIFTEDNESS (ABILITIES)

1. We can **grow** our spiritual gifts. "Desire earnestly the best gifts" (1 Corinthians 12:31).

   a. **Intensity**: to use all gifts more effectively.

   b. **Variety**: to manifest different gifts.

2. Each has an **identifying** gift. "Everyone has his proper gift" (1 Corinthians 7:7).

3. All have all gifts **embryonically**:

   a. The gift is the Holy Spirit and **all believers have Him** (see Romans 8:4).

   b. The Bible commands us to do all ministries. God wouldn't give us a responsibility without the **ability**.

4. Faith to use your unique gifts to do **different tasks**. "Having then different expressions of faith according to the gifts that are given to us" (Romans 12:3,5, ELT).

C. THE TASK OF FAITH

1. <u>Evangelism</u>

   a. Faith is **obedience** to God's command.

   b. Church **outreach**. "Go ... make disciples of all ethnic groups" (Matthew 28:19, ELT).

   c. **Individuals**. "He that winneth souls is wise" (Proverbs 11:30, KJV).

   d. Billy Graham and soul winners

2. <u>Serving</u> or ministering to people (*dikonia*)

   a. Faith to see God work **in others**.

   b. "Or ministry, let us use it [faith] in our ministering" (Romans 12:7). "God has appointed these in the church ... helps" (1 Corinthians 12:28).

   c. Ushers, deacons, women's ministry

3. <u>Counseling</u> or mercy showing

   a. Faith to see God work through sympathy, empathy, or **mentoring**.

   b. "He that showeth mercy" (Romans 12:8).

   c. Counselors, women's ministry

4. <u>Teaching</u> or Bible explanation

   a. The passion to **study** to know and **share** truth from Scripture.

   b. "God hath dealt the measure of faith ... on teaching" (Romans 12:3,7). "And He gave some ... teachers" (Ephesians 4:11). "Though I have the gift ... and understand all knowledge and all mysteries and though I have all faith" (1 Corinthians 13:2).

   c. Uses faith for spiritual illumination of Scripture, both to **know and to share**.

5. <u>Exhortation</u> and encouragement

   a. **Positive and practical**. Faith to encourage people to overcome difficulties and live for God.

   b. "God hath dealt ... the measure of faith ... he that exhorteth" (Romans 12:3,8, KJV).

6. **Prophecy**, correction, warning, rebuke, preaching

   a. To be jealous for God's **reputation** and His **law**.

   b. "Let us prophesy according to the proportion of faith" (Romans 12:3,6).

7. <u>Shepherding</u>, pastoring, leading

   a. Includes pastors and those who do **pastoring tasks**.

   b. "And he gave some ... pastors and teachers" (Ephesians 4:11).

   c. Faith to see God's work in a corporate **congregation** and in **individuals**.

   d. A Sunday school teacher is the **extension** of the pastor's ministry into the life of the class.

8. <u>Administration</u>, managing, directing

   a. Faith to use the **right person** in the right place at the right time, to do the right job in the right way.

   b. "God hath dealt the measure of faith . . . he that ruleth" (Romans 12:3,8, KJV) "governments" (1 Corinthians 12:28).

9. <u>Giving</u>, supporting

   a. Faith to give money to accomplish **God's purpose**.

   b. "God hath dealt the measure of faith ... he that giveth" (Romans 12:3,8, KJV).

10. <u>Overcome obstacles</u>, property, and things

    a. Faith to eliminate obstacles that hinder the **work of God**.

    b. "Though I have all faith ... to remove mountains (1 Corinthians 13:2). "If you have faith as a grain of mustard seed, ye shall say unto this mountain, remove ... it shall remove" (Matthew 17:20).

11. <u>Pain</u>, suffering, affliction

    a. Faith to **glorify God** through suffering.

    b. "The trial of your faith" (1 Peter 1:7). "Trying of your faith" (James 1:3).

12. <u>Martyrdom</u>, persecution

    a. Faith to glorify God when **persecuted**.

    b. "Blessed are you when they revile and persecute you, and say all kinds of evil against you falsely for My sake" (Matthew 5:11).

APPLICATION OF FAITH

1. To have a **vision/dream** of task.

2. To make **life-changing** decisions.

3. To become **intimate** with God.

4. To manage your **time, talent, and treasures** for God.

Lesson 5:

FAITH TO USE SPIRITUAL GIFTS

A. MANY PURPOSED FOR FAITH

1. Get more faith. "From faith to faith" (Romans 1:17).

   a. _____ : you get more faith.

   b. _____ : you get different kinds of faith.

2. When faith is _____ : "Oh, you of little faith" (Matthew 14:31).

3. When faith is _____ : "Weak in faith" (Romans 14:1).

4. Most believers have faith for a few tasks, but not

   _____ .

B. FAITH ACCORDING TO OUR SPIRITUAL GIFTEDNESS (ABILITIES)

1. We can _____ our spiritual gifts. "Desire earnestly the best gifts" (1 Corinthians 12:31).

   a. _____ : to use all gifts more effectively.

   b. _____ : to manifest different gifts.

2. Each has an _____ gift. "Everyone has his proper gift" (1 Corinthians 7:7).

3. All have all gifts _____ :

   a. The gift is the Holy Spirit and _____ (see Romans 8:4).

   b. The Bible commands us to do all ministries. God wouldn't give us a responsibility without the _____ .

4. Faith to use your unique gifts to do _____ . "Having then different expressions of faith according to the gifts that are given to us" (Romans 12:3,5, ELT).

C. THE TASK OF FAITH

1. _____

   a. Faith is _____ to God's command.

   b. Church _____ . "Go ... make disciples of all ethnic groups" (Matthew 28:19, ELT).

   c. _____ . "He that winneth souls is wise" (Proverbs 11:30, KJV).

   d. Billy Graham and soul winners

2. _____ or ministering to people (*dikonia*)

   a. Faith to see God work _____ .

   b. "Or ministry, let us use it [faith] in our ministering" (Romans 12:7). "God has appointed these in the church ... helps" (1 Corinthians 12:28).

   c. Ushers, deacons, women's ministry

3. _____ or mercy showing

   a. Faith to see God work through sympathy, empathy, or _____ .

   b. "He that showeth mercy" (Romans 12:8).

   c. Counselors, women's ministry

4. _____ or Bible explanation

a. The passion to _____ to know and
_____ truth from Scripture.

b. "God hath dealt the measure of faith ... on teaching" (Romans 12:3,7). "And He gave some ... teachers" (Ephesians 4:11). "Though I have the gift ... and understand all knowledge and all mysteries and though I have all faith" (1 Corinthians 13:2).

c. Uses faith for spiritual illumination of Scripture, both to

_____ .

5. _____ and encouragement

a. _____ . Faith to encourage people to overcome difficulties and live for God.

b. "God hath dealt ... the measure of faith ... he that exhorteth" (Romans 12:3,8, KJV).

6. _____ , correction, warning, rebuke, preaching

a. To be jealous for God's _____ and His _____ .

b. "Let us prophesy according to the proportion of faith" (Romans 12:3,6).

7. _____ , pastoring, leading

a. Includes pastors and those who do _____ .

b. "And he gave some ... pastors and teachers" (Ephesians 4:11).

c. Faith to see God's work in a corporate _____ and in _____ .

d. A Sunday school teacher is the _____ of the pastor's ministry into the life of the class.

8. _____ , managing, directing

    a. Faith to use the _____ in the right place at the right time, to do the right job in the right way.

    b. "God hath dealt the measure of faith . . . he that ruleth" (Romans 12:3,8, KJV) "governments" (1 Corinthians 12:28).

9. _____ , supporting

    a. Faith to give money to accomplish _____ .

    b. "God hath dealt the measure of faith ... he that giveth" (Romans 12:3,8, KJV).

10. _____ , property, and things

    a. Faith to eliminate obstacles that hinder the

    _____ .

    b. "Though I have all faith ... to remove mountains (1 Corinthians 13:2). "If you have faith as a grain of mustard seed, ye shall say unto this mountain, remove ... it shall remove" (Matthew 17:20).

11. _____ , suffering, affliction

    a. Faith to _____ through suffering.

    b. "The trial of your faith" (1 Peter 1:7). "Trying of your faith" (James 1:3).

12. _____ , persecution

    a. Faith to glorify God when _____ .

    b. "Blessed are you when they revile and persecute you, and say all kinds of evil against you falsely for My sake" (Matthew 5:11).

APPLICATION OF FAITH

1. To have a _____ of task.

2. To make _____ decisions.

3. To become _____ with God.

4. To manage your _____ for God.

Lesson 6:

THINGS THAT HINDER/WEAKEN FAITH

A. REVIEW LESSONS ON FAITH

1. Faith is a **relationship**. "Have faith in God" (Mark 11:22).

2. It takes **two wings to fly**. "Faith without works is dead" (James 2:20).

3. Your faith **can grow**. "From faith to faith" (Romans 1:17).

4. Different believers express faith for **different purposes**. "Having then different expressions of faith ... according to the gifts that are given to us" (Romans 12:3,5, ELT).

B. ILLUSTRATIONS OF WEAK FAITH

1. **Abraham**. "Weak in faith" (Romans 4:19).

2. **Peter**. "O, you of little faith" (Matthew 14:31).

3. **Legalistic** believers. "One who is weak in the faith" (Romans 14:1).

4. Faithlessness is **neutral**. "Be not faithless" (John 20:27).

5. **Doubt**, *dialogia*. "But some doubted" (Matthew 28:17).

6. **Unbelief**. "Help thou mine unbelief" (Mark 9:24).

C. 20 STEPS THAT WEAKEN FAITH

1. Know **unconfessed** sin. "If I regard iniquity in my heart, the Lord will not hear me" (Psalm 66:18).

2. Sin of **ignorance**. This comes from ignorance of Scripture, lack of growth, or lack of seeking God.

3. **Dead faith**. "Even so faith is dead" (James 2:17).

4. Wrong **motive**. "You receive not ... because you spend it upon your pleasures" (James 4:3, ELT).

5. Not doing the **right thing**. "To him that knoweth to do good, and doeth it not, to him it is sin" (James 4:17, KJV).

6. Not **walking with God**. "Draw near to God, and He will draw near to you" (James 4:8).

7. Being **drawn away by satan**. "Resist the devil and he will flee from you" (James 4:7).

8. Haven't acted in **true faith**. "You have not because you ask not" (James 4:2).

9. Harboring **idols**. "Little children, keep yourselves from idols" (1 John 5:21).

10. An **unforgiving** spirit. "If you have anything against anyone, forgive him, that your Father in heaven may also forgive you" (Mark 11:25).

11. Failure to respond to the **needs of the poor**. "Whoever shuts his ears to the cry of the poor will also cry himself and not be heard" (Proverbs 21:13).

12. **Domestic conflict**. "Husbands, dwell with them according to knowledge, giving honour unto the wife, as unto the weaker vessel ... that your prayers be not hindered" (1 Peter 3:7).

13. Directing faith **in wrong directions**. "Without faith it is impossible to please God, for he that cometh to God must believe that He is, and that He is a rewarder of them that diligently seek him" (Hebrews 11:6).

"Diligently" means ...

Not I but Christ

Christ **first**

For me to live is Christ

14. Improper **reverence**. "He will fulfill the desire of them that fear him, he will hear their cry" (Psalm 145:19).

15. Not sincere and pray with great **intensity**. "Do it heartily, as to the Lord" (Colossians 3:23). "Laboring fervently for you in prayers" (Colossians 4:12).

16. **Not agree** with others in prayer. "If two of you shall agree on earth as touching anything that they shall ask, it shall be done for them" (Matthew 18:19).

There is value in the volume of prayer

17. Not **abiding** in Scripture. "If you abide in Me, and My words abide in you, you shall ask what you will" (John 15:7).

18. **Spiritually blinded** by satan. "The god of this world has blinded the minds" (2 Corinthians 4:4).

19. Giving up **too soon**. "Continue in prayer" (Colossians 4:2). "Pray without ceasing" (1 Thessalonians 5:17).

20. Giving in to the **old nature**. "The spirit is willing, but the flesh is weak" (Matthew 26:41).

Lesson 6:

QUESTIONS

THINGS THAT HINDER/WEAKEN FAITH

A. REVIEW LESSONS ON FAITH

1. Faith is a _____ . "Have faith in God" (Mark 11:22).

2. It takes _____ . "Faith without works is dead" (James 2:20).

3. Your faith _____ . "From faith to faith" (Romans 1:17).

4. Different believers express faith for _____ . "Having then different expressions of faith ... according to the gifts that are given to us" (Romans 12:3,5, ELT).

B. ILLUSTRATIONS OF WEAK FAITH

1. _____ . "Weak in faith" (Romans 4:19).

2. _____ . "O, you of little faith" (Matthew 14:31).

3. _____ believers. "One who is weak in the faith" (Romans 14:1).

4. Faithlessness is _____ . "Be not faithless" (John 20:27).

5. _____ , *dialogia*. "But some doubted" (Matthew 28:17).

6. _____ . "Help thou mine unbelief" (Mark 9:24).

C. 20 STEPS THAT WEAKEN FAITH

1. Know _____ sin. "If I regard iniquity in my heart, the Lord will not hear me" (Psalm 66:18).

2. Sin of_____ . This comes from ignorance of Scripture, lack of growth, or lack of seeking God.

3. _____ . "Even so faith is dead" (James 2:17).

4. Wrong_____ . "You receive not ... because you spend it upon your pleasures" (James 4:3, ELT).

5. Not doing the _____ . "To him that knoweth to do good, and doeth it not, to him it is sin" (James 4:17, KJV).

6. Not _____ . "Draw near to God, and He will draw near to you" (James 4:8).

7. Being _____ . "Resist the devil and he will flee from you" (James 4:7).

8. Haven't acted in _____ . "You have not because you ask not" (James 4:2).

9. Harboring _____ . "Little children, keep yourselves from idols" (1 John 5:21).

10. An _____ spirit. "If you have anything against anyone, forgive him, that your Father in heaven may also forgive you" (Mark 11:25).

11. Failure to respond to the _____ . "Whoever shuts his ears to the cry of the poor will also cry himself and not be heard" (Proverbs 21:13).

12. _____ . "Husbands, dwell with them according to knowledge, giving honour unto the wife, as unto the weaker vessel ... that your prayers be not hindered" (1 Peter 3:7).

13. Directing faith _____ . "Without faith it is impossible to please God, for he that cometh to God must believe that He is, and that He is a rewarder of them that diligently seek him" (Hebrews 11:6).

"Diligently" means …

_____ Christ

Christ _____

_____ Christ

14. Improper _____ . "He will fulfill the desire of them that fear him, he will hear their cry" (Psalm 145:19).

15. Not sincere and pray with great _____ . "Do it heartily, as to the Lord" (Colossians 3:23). "Laboring fervently for you in prayers" (Colossians 4:12).

16. _____ with others in prayer. "If two of you shall agree on earth as touching anything that they shall ask, it shall be done for them" (Matthew 18:19).

There is value in the volume of prayer

17. Not _____ in Scripture. "If you abide in Me, and My words abide in you, you shall ask what you will" (John 15:7).

18. _____ by satan. "The god of this world has blinded the minds" (2 Corinthians 4:4).

19. Giving up _____ . "Continue in prayer" (Colossians 4:2). "Pray without ceasing" (1 Thessalonians 5:17).

20. Giving in to the _____ . "The spirit is willing, but the flesh is weak" (Matthew 26:41).

Lesson 7:

ANSWER KEY

HOW TO GROW YOUR FAITH

A. INTRODUCTION

"Your faith groweth exceedingly" (2 Thessalonians 1:3, KJV).

1. From **seed faith**. "Faith as a grain of mustard seed" (Matthew 17:20).

    a. Grow your **little faith**. "O you of little faith" (Matthew 14:31).

    b. Grow your **weak faith**. "Weak in faith" (Romans 14:1).

    c. Grow your **strong faith**. "Abraham ... was strong in faith" (Romans 14:20).

2. **Growth in faith** is a possibility. "Your faith groweth exceedingly" (2 Thessalonians 1:3, KJV).

3. The phrase "from faith to faith" (Romans 1:17).

    a. From **saving** faith to walking by faith.

    b. From **doctrinal** faith to living by faith.

    c. Grow from understanding faith to **living by faith**.

    d. First seeking faith to the **assurance of faith**.

B. 10 PRINCIPLES TO GROW YOUR FAITH

1. **By prayer**. "Lord, increase our faith" (Luke 17:5).

   a. Pray to **learn** what to do in service.

   b. Pray for **insight** to learn the Word.

   c. Pray for **discipline** that leads to holiness and worship.

   d. Pray for **experiences** that will stretch your faith.

   e. Pray for **courage and wisdom** to take a leap of faith.

2. By the Word of God. "Faith cometh by hearing ... the Word of God" (Romans 10:13).

   a. **Hear**—small pinky (see Revelation 1:3).

   b. **Read**—ring man (see Revelation 1:3).

   c. **Study**—tall man (see 2 Timothy 2:15).

   d. **Memorize**—pointer (see Psalm 119:11).

   e. **Meditate**—thumb (see 1 Timothy 4:15; Psalm 1:3).

3. By obedience and exercise. "Oh you of little faith" (Matthew 14:31).

   a. How to get strong muscles? **Exercise**.

   b. How to stay on an exercise routine? **Obedience**.

   c. Effective exercise is:

      i. Regular

      ii. Repetitive

      iii. Stretching

      iv. Increasing in strength

4. By looking to Jesus. "Looking unto Jesus, the author and finisher of our faith" (Hebrews 12:1).

   a. How do we walk? Keep **eyes** on Jesus.

   b. Walk according to **Scripture**. "But if we walk in the light ... the blood of Jesus Christ His Son cleanses us from all sin" (1 John 1:7).

   c. Don't focus on **problems and obstacles**. "When he [Peter] saw the wind was boisterous" (Matthew 14:30).

5. By the indwelling Christ. "I am crucified with Christ, nevertheless I am still alive. I live by the indwelling Christ in me, who gives me His life and faith to live for Him" (Galatians 2:20, ELT).

6. By seeking the Lord. **Intimacy**. "When You said, 'Seek My face,' My heart said to You, 'Your face, Lord, I will seek'" (Psalm 27:8). How do you seek? **Continuous action**. "Ask, and it will be given to you; seek, and you will find; knock, and it will be opened to you" (Matthew 7:7).

7. By constant cleansing of the blood of Christ. "If we walk in the light ... the blood of Jesus ... cleanseth from all sin" (1 John 1:7).

   a. Condition one: **light-walking**.

   b. Condition two: **recognize our sin**.

   c. Condition three: confess and forsake sin.

WHAT TO DO WITH YOUR SIN

Confess it **to God**.

Repent and **not do it again**.

Learn from it.

Become **wiser and closer** to God.

1. By not trusting in yourself.

   a. **Dead faith**. "Faith without works is dead" (James 2:20), i.e., good works.

   b. It takes two wings to fly, which is **faith and obedience**.

2. By surrendering to God.

   a. Live by "the faith of Christ," not by **your faith** (Galatians 2:20).

   b. "Our faith gives us victory to overcome the world" (1 John 5:4).

3. By gratitude.

    a. Thanksgiving **grows** our faith. "So, walk in Him ... established in the faith ... with thanksgiving" (Colossians 2:6-7).

    b. Why does gratitude strengthen faith? It turns **all energies to God**.

Lesson 7:

HOW TO GROW YOUR FAITH

A. INTRODUCTION

"Your faith groweth exceedingly" (2 Thessalonians 1:3, KJV).

1. From _____ . "Faith as a grain of mustard seed" (Matthew 17:20).

   a. Grow your _____ . "O you of little faith" (Matthew 14:31).

   b. Grow your _____ . "Weak in faith" (Romans 14:1).

   c. Grow your _____ . "Abraham ... was strong in faith" (Romans 14:20).

2. _____ is a possibility. "Your faith groweth exceedingly" (2 Thessalonians 1:3, KJV).

3. The phrase "from faith to faith" (Romans 1:17).

   a. From _____ faith to walking by faith.

   b. From _____ faith to living by faith.

c. Grow from understanding faith to _____ .

d. First seeking faith to the _____ .

B. 10 PRINCIPLES TO GROW YOUR FAITH

1. _____ . "Lord, increase our faith" (Luke 17:5).

    a. Pray to _____ what to do in service.

    b. Pray for _____ to learn the Word.

    c. Pray for _____ that leads to holiness and worship.

    d. Pray for _____ that will stretch your faith.

    e. Pray for _____ to take a leap of faith.

2. By the Word of God. "Faith cometh by hearing ... the Word of God" (Romans 10:13).

    a. _____ —small pinky (see Revelation 1:3).

    b. _____ —ring man (see Revelation 1:3).

    c. _____ —tall man (see 2 Timothy 2:15).

    d. _____ —pointer (see Psalm 119:11).

    e. _____ —thumb (see 1 Timothy 4:15; Psalm 1:3).

3. By obedience and exercise. "Oh you of little faith" (Matthew 14:31).

   a. How to get strong muscles? _____ .

   b. How to stay on an exercise routine? _____ .

   c. Effective exercise is:

      i. Regular

      ii. Repetitive

      iii. Stretching

      iv. Increasing in strength

4. By looking to Jesus. "Looking unto Jesus, the author and finisher of our faith" (Hebrews 12:1).

   a. How do we walk? Keep _____ on Jesus.

   b. Walk according to _____ . "But if we walk in the light ... the blood of Jesus Christ His Son cleanses us from all sin" (1 John 1:7).

   c. Don't focus on _____ . "When he [Peter] saw the wind was boisterous" (Matthew 14:30).

5. By the indwelling Christ. "I am crucified with Christ, nevertheless I am still alive. I live by the indwelling Christ in me, who gives me His life and faith to live for Him" (Galatians 2:20, ELT).

6. By seeking the Lord. _____ . "When You said, 'Seek My face,' My heart said to You, 'Your face, Lord, I will seek'" (Psalm 27:8). How do you seek? _____ . "Ask, and it will be given to you; seek, and you will find; knock, and it will be opened to you" (Matthew 7:7).

7. By constant cleansing of the blood of Christ. "If we walk in the light ... the blood of Jesus ... cleanseth from all sin" (1 John 1:7).

   a. Condition one: _____ .

   b. Condition two: _____ .

   c. Condition three: confess and forsake sin.

WHAT TO DO WITH YOUR SIN

Confess it _____ .

Repent and _____ .

_____ from it.

Become _____ to God.

1. By not trusting in yourself.

   a. _____ . "Faith without works is dead" (James 2:20), i.e., good works.

   b. It takes two wings to fly, which is _____ .

2. By surrendering to God.

   a. Live by "the faith of Christ," not by _____ (Galatians 2:20).

   b. "Our faith gives us victory to overcome the world" (1 John 5:4).

3. By gratitude.

    a. Thanksgiving _____ our faith. "So, walk
       in Him ... established in the faith ... with thanksgiving"
       (Colossians 2:6-7).

    b. Why does gratitude strengthen faith? It turns

       _____ .

PART FOUR

FAITH
WALKING
through
PROBLEMS

ADDITIONAL RESOURCES

POWERPOINT SLIDES:

To purchase and download the Powerpoint Slides go to
https://www.norimediagroup.com/pages/elmer-towns

VIDEO:

To purchase available video by Dr. Towns go to
https://www.norimediagroup.com/pages/elmer-towns

ADD-ON CONTENT

To purchase additional products in this series go to
https://www.norimediagroup.com/pages/elmer-towns

RELATED BOOKS

My Name is the Holy Spirit: Discover Me through My Name
Available at https://www.norimediagroup.com/pages/elmer-towns

www.ingramcontent.com/pod-product-compliance
Lightning Source LLC
Chambersburg PA
CBHW060014100426
42740CB00010B/1487